ECHOES OF SORROW: GAZA GENOCIDE THROUGH EGYPTIAN EYES

BY OMAR IBRAHIM

Echoes of Sorrow: Gaza Genocide Through Egyptian Eyes

A Collection of Blogs Written During the Genocide

by Omar Ibrahim

CONTENTS

CONTENTS

CONTENTS

ECHOES OF RESISTANCE: COMPARING THE YOM KIPPUR WAR AND HAMAS' QUEST FOR PALESTINIAN FREEDOM

THE ISRAELI-PALESTINIAN CONFLICT, WHICH HAS BEEN ONGOING SINCE THE MIDDLE OF THE 20TH CENTURY, IS CONSIDERED ONE OF THE WORLD'S LONGEST-LASTING CONFLICTS. NUMEROUS ATTEMPTS HAVE BEEN MADE TO RESOLVE THIS CONFLICT, BOTH AS PART OF THE ISRAELI-PALESTINIAN PEACE PROCESS AND IN CONJUNCTION WITH EFFORTS TO ADDRESS THE BROADER ARAB-ISRAELI CONFLICT. THE REGION HAS EXPERIENCED TENSIONS DATING BACK TO THE LATE 19TH AND EARLY 20TH CENTURIES, WITH PUBLIC CLAIMS MADE FOR A JEWISH HOMELAND IN PALESTINE, SUCH AS THE FIRST ZIONIST CONGRESS OF 1897 AND THE BALFOUR DECLARATION OF 1917, LEADING TO INCREASED TENSIONS DUE TO WAVES OF JEWISH IMMIGRATION. FOLLOWING WORLD WAR I, THE MANDATE FOR PALESTINE INCLUDED A COMMITMENT TO ESTABLISHING

ECHOES OF RESISTANCE: COMPARING THE YOM KIPPUR WAR AND HAMAS' QUEST FOR PALESTINIAN FREEDOM

A NATIONAL HOME FOR THE JEWISH PEOPLE. THESE TENSIONS EVENTUALLY ESCALATED INTO OPEN SECTARIAN CONFLICT BETWEEN JEWS AND ARABS. DESPITE THE 1947 UNITED NATIONS PARTITION PLAN FOR PALESTINE, WHICH WAS NEVER PUT INTO EFFECT. SEVERAL WARS IGNITD THE CONFLICT, MOST NOTABLY IN 1948–49, 1956, 1967, 1973, 1982, 2006, AND THE FULL WAR STARTED YESTERDAY IGNITED BY HAMAS.

YET, THE WAR IGNITED YESTERDAY HAS A LOT OF SIMILARTIES WITH THE 1973 WAR, WHICH WILL BE DISCUSSED THOROUGHLY NEXT.

THE YOM KIPPUR WAR

THE YOM KIPPUR WAR, ALSO REFERRED TO AS THE RAMADAN WAR, THE OCTOBER WAR, THE 1973 ARAB-ISRAELI WAR, OR THE FOURTH ARAB-ISRAELI WAR, OCCURRED BETWEEN OCTOBER 6 AND 25, 1973. IT WAS A CONFLICT BETWEEN ISRAEL AND A COALITION OF ARAB STATES LED BY EGYPT AND SYRIA. THE MAIN BATTLEGROUNDS WERE THE SINAI PENINSULA AND THE GOLAN HEIGHTS, BOTH OF WHICH HAD BEEN OCCUPIED BY ISRAEL SINCE 1967.

SOME FIGHTING ALSO TOOK PLACE IN AFRICAN EGYPT AND NORTHERN ISRAEL. EGYPT'S INITIAL GOAL IN THE WAR WAS TO GAIN CONTROL OF THE EASTERN BANK OF THE SUEZ CANAL AND SUBSEQUENTLY USE THIS AS LEVERAGE TO NEGOTIATE THE RETURN OF THE REST OF THE ISRAELI-OCCUPIED SINAI PENINSULA

OPERATION AL-AQSA FLOOD

YESTERDAY, ON OCTOBER 6, 2023, LOOKING AHEAD TO EXACTLY 50 YEARS LATER, ISRAEL EXPERIENCED A BARRAGE OF OVER 5,000 ROCKETS. THE GAZA-BASED HAMAS GROUP DECLARED THE START OF 'OPERATION AL-AQSA FLOOD', URGING "RESISTANCE FIGHTERS IN THE WEST BANK" AND INDIVIDUALS FROM "ARAB AND ISLAMIC NATIONS" TO JOIN THE FIGHT AGAINST ISRAEL, WHICH THEY ACCUSE OF "ILLEGALLY OCCUPYING" PALESTINIAN TERRITORY.

HAMAS OFFICIALS ATTRIBUTE THE RECENT OUTBREAK OF VIOLENCE TO LONGSTANDING TENSIONS BETWEEN ISRAEL AND PALESTINIANS, SPECIFICALLY THE ONGOING DISPUTE

ECHOES OF RESISTANCE: COMPARING THE YOM KIPPUR WAR AND HAMAS' QUEST FOR PALESTINIAN FREEDOM

CONCERNING THE SACRED AL-AQSA MOSQUE COMPOUND. THIS SITE HOLDS SIGNIFICANT REVERENCE FOR BOTH MUSLIMS AND JEWS, AND HAS A HISTORY FILLED WITH VIOLENCE, INCLUDING THE INTENSE 11-DAY WAR BETWEEN ISRAEL AND HAMAS IN 2021.

THE ISRAELI SHOCK, OCCURRING ON SIMCHAT TORAH, ONE OF THE HOLIEST DAYS IN JUDAISM, BORE SIMILARITIES TO THE UNEXPECTED ATTACK THAT MARKED THE BEGINNING OF THE YOM KIPPUR WAR IN 1973.

ON THIS DAY, WHICH HAS DOUBLE-SIGNIFICANCE AS BEING BOTH HOLY IN JUDAISM AND THE 50TH ANNIVERSARY OF THE 1973 CONFLICT, HAMAS MADE A SELECTION THAT WAS NOTED BY THE ISRAELI MEDIA. IN THE DAYS LEADING UP TO THIS, THE YOM KIPPUR WAR WAS REMEMBERED, AND A LOT OF ISRAELIS VIEWED SIMILARITIES BETWEEN THE CURRENT STRUGGLE AND THE EVENTS OF YEARS BEFORE.

AS ISRAELIS WERE READY TO ENJOY SIMCHAT TORAH, HAMAS LAUNCHED THOUSANDS OF MISSILES COUPLED WITH A DARING LAND-SEA-AIR ASSAULT WHICH KILLED MANY, TURNING THE OCCASION INTO A TRAGEDY FOR THE ISRAELIS.

ECHOES OF RESISTANCE: COMPARING THE YOM KIPPUR WAR AND HAMAS' QUEST FOR PALESTINIAN FREEDOM

IN RESPONSE TO THE AGGRESSION BY HAMAS, PRIME MINISTER BENJAMIN NETANYAHU OF ISRAEL DECLARED A STATE OF WAR AND INITIATED A MILITARY CAMPAIGN AGAINST THE PALESTINIAN ORGANIZATION, ESPECIALLY IN THE GAZA STRIP AREA.

HAMAS HAS URGED THEIR COMBATANTS IN THE WEST BANK, AS WELL AS OTHER ARABS AND MUSLIMS, TO JOIN THE FRAY AGAINST ISRAEL. THE CURRENT DISPUTE BETWEEN ISRAELIS AND PALESTINIANS IN EAST JERUSALEM, GAZA, AND THE WEST BANK HAVE LEFT TENSIONS RUNNING HIGH.

ISRAEL'S MILITARY AND INTELLIGENCE FAILURE: ANALYZING ISRAEL'S PREPARATION FOR THE "WRONG WAR"

FOR THREE YEARS, ISRAEL CONSTRUCTED A FORTIFIED BORDER FENCE AROUND THE GAZA STRIP WITH SOPHISTICATED SECURITY FEATURES SUCH AS SENSORS AND A RADAR THAT COULD DETECT EVEN CRAWLING ANTS.

ON SATURDAY, HOWEVER, HAMAS MILITANTS MANAGED TO BREACH THE BARRIER WITH VEHICLES, BOATS, AND AUTOMATED GLIDERS, BULLDOZERS, AND ATTACKED MILITARY TARGETS AND CIVILIANS IN SOUTHERN ISRAEL, MARKING THE BIGGEST MILITARY INFILTRATION SINCE THE 1973 "SIX-DAY WAR" - A MAJOR MILITARY AND INTELLIGENCE FAILURE ACCORDING TO THE WALL STREET JOURNAL. THE NEWSPAPER ASSERTED THAT THIS HIGHLIGHTED THE ISRAELI ARMY'S FOCUS ON CYBER CAPABILITIES, INTELLIGENCE GATHERING, AND ADVANCED WEAPONRY THAT WAS DEEMED FUTILE TO COUNTER HAMAS'S ATTACKS, AND IT ALSO HIGHLIGHTED ISRAEL'S SURPRISE AT THE "LOW-TECH" GROUND ASSAULT.

ISRAEL'S MILITARY AND INTELLIGENCE FAILURE: ANALYZING ISRAEL'S PREPARATION FOR THE "WRONG WAR"

IN RESPONSE, THE ISRAELI ARMY IS PREPARING FOR A LARGE-SCALE OPERATION IN GAZA WHERE THEY WILL HAVE TO UTILIZE TRADITIONAL INFANTRY AND ARTILLERY TEAMS, AREAS WHICH HAD NOT BEEN PRIORITIZED IN RECENT YEARS AND MAY RESULT IN STREET WARFARE. AVI JAGER, A RESEARCHER AT THE INTERNATIONAL COUNTERTERRORISM INSTITUTE BASED IN ISRAEL, CLAIMED "THE ISRAELI ARMY WAS PREPARING FOR THE WRONG WAR." THEIR FOCUS HAD BEEN ON THE WEST BANK, DEPLOYING FORCES TO QUASH PALESTINIAN FACTIONS AND INTELLIGENCE WARNINGS POINTING TO THE ISRAELI NORTH (SOUTHERN LEBANON) AND THE THREAT POSED BY THE LEBANESE HEZBOLLAH, AN ALLY OF HAMAS.

UNTIL SATURDAY, OFFICIALS BELIEVED THAT THE POLICY OF BOOSTING GAZA'S ECONOMY MEANT THAT HAMAS LEADERS HAD NO INTEREST IN LAUNCHING THIS TYPE OF ATTACK. THE IZZ AL-DIN AL-QASSAM BRIGADES, THE MILITARY WING OF HAMAS, NEVERTHELESS LAUNCHED A NEVER-SEEN-BEFORE ATTACK ON ISRAEL BY AIR, SEA AND LAND. DANIEL LEVY, THE FORMER ISRAELI NEGOTIATOR WITH

THE PALESTINIANS AND HEAD OF THE UNITED STATES/MIDDLE EAST PROJECT, COMMENTED THAT "ISRAEL HAS SUFFERED A STRATEGIC SURPRISE, DESPITE ITS ADVANCED TECHNOLOGIES, , WEAPONS, SPYWARE, AND WORLD-RENOWNED INTELLIGENCE AGENCY."

IN REGARDS TO ENDING THE ISRAELI-PALESTINIAN CONFLICT, HE CLAIMED "ISRAEL CANNOT MAINTAIN THE SAFETY OF ITS PEOPLE ANYMORE - AND IT WILL BE DIFFICULT TO RECOVER FROM THAT." AS THE WALL STREET JOURNAL HIGHLIGHTED, "WHILE ISRAEL HAS LONG FOCUSED ON GAINING A TECHNOLOGICAL ADVANTAGE OVER ITS ENEMIES, THE ISRAELI ARMY ALWAYS FOCUSED ON SEARCHING FOR ADVANCED AIR, DEFENSE AND INTELLIGENCE SYSTEMS OVER THE PAST TWO DECADES." TO DEAL WITH THE THREAT POSED BY HEZBOLLAH AND HAMAS, THE MILITARY INVESTED IN INTELLIGENCE, CYBER, AND DEFENSE CAPABILITIES AND DEPLOYED THE IRON DOME SYSTEM IN 2011, WHICH TARGETS SHORT-RANGE MISSILES.

AS IRAN ENTERED THE SYRIAN CIVIL WAR, ISRAELI PILOTS CONDUCTED THOUSANDS OF AIR STRIKES IN SYRIA TO IMPEDE

ISRAEL'S MILITARY AND INTELLIGENCE FAILURE: ANALYZING ISRAEL'S PREPARATION FOR THE "WRONG WAR"

TEHRAN'S EFFORTS TO SUPPLY ITS ALLY IN LEBANON, HEZBOLLAH, WITH ADVANCED MISSILES. ITS WORTH MENTIONING THAT ONE OF ITS MEANS TO COUNTER HAMAS, THE ISRAELI MILITARY RESORTED TO TECHNOLOGY BY CREATING THE "OQABA" SYSTEM WHICH COULD DETECT TUNNELS, AND LATER UNVEILED THE BORDER FENCE SYSTEM. IN 2015, THE ARMY BEGAN WORKING ON A RENEWAL PLAN THAT WOULD REDUCE COMBAT FORCES AND RESERVISTS.

HAMAS, WHO HAS CONTROLLED THE GAZA STRIP FOR MORE THAN A DECADE, MEANWHILE BUILT A GROUP OF UNDERGROUND BASES TO SERVE AS A COMMAND AND CONTROL CENTER IN ANY FUTURE CONFLICT, AND BECAME MORE ACCURATE IN LAUNCHING ROCKETS AT ISRAEL.

FINALLY, IT WILL BE INTERESTING TO SEE HOW THE CONFLICT WILL END, THE ISRAELI PRIME MINISTER HAS STATED THAT ISRAEL WILL CHANGE THE ENTIRE MIDDLE EAST MAP DUE TO THESE ATTACKS, WITH SUSPICION THAT ISRAEL WANTS TO REVIVE OLD PLANS TO MOVE THE ENTIRE GAZAN POPULATION TO SINAI, EGYPT. SOMETHING THAT WILL NOT BE ACCEPTED BY THE EGYPTIAN COUNTERPART,

ISRAEL'S MILITARY AND INTELLIGENCE FAILURE: ANALYZING ISRAEL'S PREPARATION FOR THE "WRONG WAR"

IT IS PRECIEVED EVEN THAT A LAND INCURSION ON GAZA BY ISRAELI FORCES WILL BE VETOED BY EGYPT, DUE TO ITS IMPLICATIONS ON EGYPTIAN NATIONAL SECURITY.

IF ISRAEL INSISTS ON THESE PLANS, IT CAN RISK THE EXPANSION OF THE CURRENT WAR, AND IT SHOULD CALCULATE THAT IF IT CAN NOT HANDLE HAMAS, OR HEZBOLLAH, OR EVEN THE MILITIAS IN SYRIA, CAN IT REALLY HANDLE A MODERNIZED EGYPTIAN ARMY? IT SHOULD ALSO BEAR IN MIND THE FURTHER REACTIONS OF THE NEARBY ARAB GULF STATES, WHO WILL NOT ALLOW THE CONFLICT TO EXPAND FURTHER WITHOUT SERIOUS REPERCUSIONS.

Unraveling the Forgotten Chapters: Origins of the Palestinian Cause

Many believe that the root cause of the problems in the Middle East over the past hundred years is the occuption of Palestine, which is considered a central and significant issue. It may temporarily fade from the Arab political agenda, but it consistently resurfaces in various forms, whether forcefully or behind the scenes, always lingering in the background of any situation.

In the Western geopolitical perspective and political imagery, this issue extends to encompass the entire Middle East. Consequently, it has become customary in Western literature and media to refer to the Arab-Israeli conflict as the Middle East crisis. Unfortunately, the international community's conscience has been gradually eroding over the years, witnessing the documented rights of Palestinians being disregarded under numerous United Nations resolutions. The legitimacy granted

BY THESE RESOLUTIONS SEEMS TO BE FUTILE. WITH NO CLEAR PROSPECTS FOR A PEACEFUL RESOLUTION AND THE CONTINUOUS EXPANSION OF ISRAELI SETTLEMENTS ENCROACHING UPON THE RIGHTS OF AN OPPRESSED PEOPLE, THE INTERNATIONAL COMMUNITY FINDS ITSELF INCAPABLE OF ENFORCING INTERNATIONAL LEGITIMACY IN A MATTER THAT HAS PERSISTED FOR MORE THAN SEVEN DECADES.

THE PALESTINIAN TRAGEDY ENCOMPASSES THE HISTORICAL AND POLITICAL CONFLICT AS WELL AS THE HUMANITARIAN CRISIS IN PALESTINE, FROM THE FIRST ZIONIST CONFERENCE IN 1897 AD UP UNTIL THE PRESENT DAY.

THE ZIONIST CONFERENCE OF 1897 WAS A CRUCIAL ELEMENT OF THE ARAB-ISRAELI CONFLICT, WHOSE RESULTS WERE THE RISE OF ZIONISM IN THE WORLD, OFFICIALLY. AND THE START OF JEWISH IMMIGRATION TO PALESTINE, LEADING TO WARS AND CRISES IN THE MIDDLE EAST REGION, ALSO THE INVOLVEMENT OF MAJOR WORLD POWERS HAS PLAYED A SIGNIFICANT ROLE IN SHAPING EVENTS IN THE REGION.

THE AMBITIONS OF THE EUROPEAN COLONIAL POWERS

DURING THE NINETEENTH CENTURY, WHEN EUROPEAN COLONIALISM ARRIVED IN ARAB LANDS, SCHOLARS AND ARCHAEOLOGISTS WERE DRAWN TO JERUSALEM AS THE BIRTHPLACE OF CHRIST AND THE LAND OF THE TORAH. THE ZIONIST MOVEMENT SAW AN OPPORTUNITY IN THIS, USING IT TO ADVOCATE FOR THE RETURN OF JEWS TO THE HOLY LAND AND CAPITALIZING ON THE AMBITIONS OF COLONIAL POWERS. IN THE EAST, THEY ESTABLISHED ASSOCIATIONS, INSTITUTIONS, AND RESEARCH SCHOOLS IN SEARCH OF EVIDENCE TO SUPPORT THEIR CLAIM TO RETURN.

IN 1881, A RUSSIAN JEWISH PHYSICIAN NAMED LEOBENSKER PROPOSED THAT JEWS SHOULD BE RELOCATED FROM THEIR COMMUNITIES TO A TERRITORY THEY OWNED, IN ORDER TO ESTABLISH A JEWISH NATION. THIS IDEA WAS FURTHER CHAMPIONED BY HERZL, WHO SELECTED PALESTINE AS THE DESIRED LOCATION BASED ON THE BELIEF THAT IT WAS THEIR ANCESTRAL HOMELAND AND THEY HAD A LEGITIMATE RIGHT TO RECLAIM IT. THIS IDEA GAINED TRACTION WITH THE SUPPORT OF THE BRITISH MANDATE.

SYKES-PICOT AGREEMENT

IN 1916, THE SYKES-PICOT AGREEMENT WAS A CLANDESTINE UNDERSTANDING BETWEEN FRANCE AND THE UNITED KINGDOM, WITH THE RUSSIAN EMPIRE'S ENDORSEMENT, TO PARTITION THE FERTILE CRESCENT REGION. THIS DIVISION AIMED TO ESTABLISH RESPECTIVE SPHERES OF INFLUENCE IN WEST ASIA FOLLOWING THE COLLAPSE OF THE OTTOMAN EMPIRE DURING WORLD WAR I.

THE AGREEMENT MATERIALIZED THROUGH COVERT NEGOTIATIONS BETWEEN FRANÇOIS-GEORGES-PICOT, A FRENCH DIPLOMAT, AND MARK SYKES, A BRITISH REPRESENTATIVE. IT INVOLVED THE EXCHANGE OF DOCUMENTS BETWEEN THE FOREIGN MINISTRIES OF FRANCE, BRITAIN, AND TSARIST RUSSIA AT THAT TIME. THE FERTILE CRESCENT REGION WAS DIVIDED AS PER THE TERMS OF THE AGREEMENT. FOLLOWING THE WAR'S CONCLUSION, THE HEADS OF GOVERNMENT IN FRANCE AND BRITAIN MADE AMENDMENTS TO THE SYKES-PICOT AGREEMENT. IN 1922, AFTER SUPPRESSING REVOLUTIONS IN PALESTINE, SYRIA, AND IRAQ, THE LEAGUE OF NATIONS OFFICIALLY APPROVED PLACING THESE AREAS UNDER FRENCH AND BRITISH MANDATES.

CERTAIN POLITICAL EXPERTS CONTEND THAT THE SYKES-PICOT TREATY, WHICH WAS SIGNED OVER A CENTURY AGO, WAS THE VERY BEGINNING OF THE DISINTEGRATION OF ARAB NATIONS. THERE IS NOW A ROBUST PROPOSAL TO RECONFIGURE THE ARAB WORLD INTO STATES BASED ON SECTARIAN ALIGNMENTS, SUCH AS A STATE SPECIFICALLY DESIGNATED FOR CHRISTIANS, ANOTHER FOR SHIITES, ALAWITES, SUNNIS, OR KURDS. THIS PROPOSAL ALSO SERVES TO ENCOURAGE ISRAEL TO ADOPT AN OFFICIALLY RECOGNIZED SECTARIAN STATUS AS THE "JEWISH STATE."

PALESTINE.. A PROMISE TO THOSE WHO HAVE NO RIGHT TO GIVE SUCH PROMISE

IN 1917, ARTHUR JAMES BALFOUR, THE BRITISH FOREIGN SECRETARY, WROTE A LETTER TO LORD ROTHSCHILD, A PROMINENT LEADER OF THE ZIONIST MOVEMENT AT THAT TIME. THIS LETTER, KNOWN AS THE BALFOUR DECLARATION, MARKED THE INITIAL EFFORTS OF THE WESTERN POWERS TO ESTABLISH A JEWISH HOMELAND IN PALESTINE. THE BRITISH GOVERNMENT MADE A COMMITMENT IN THE DECLARATION TO

SUPPORT THE ESTABLISHMENT OF A JEWISH STATE IN PALESTINE.

FOLLOWING THIS, THE BRITISH FORCES, LED BY THE RENOWNED "GENERAL THE PROPHET," ENTERED JERUSALEM ON DECEMBER 11, 1917. DURING THE VERSAILLES CONFERENCE IN JANUARY 1919, THE ZIONIST MOVEMENT PRESENTED A PLAN TO IMPLEMENT THE SETTLEMENT PROJECT IN PALESTINE. THEY ALSO CALLED FOR BRITISH SUPERVISION IN ORDER TO CARRY OUT THE OBJECTIVES OF THE BALFOUR DECLARATION. PRIOR TO ITS PUBLICATION, THE AMERICAN PRESIDENT WILSON REVIEWED AND APPROVED THE CONTENT OF THE BALFOUR DECLARATION. FRANCE AND ITALY ALSO GAVE THEIR OFFICIAL APPROVAL IN 1918, FOLLOWED BY AN OFFICIAL ENDORSEMENT FROM PRESIDENT WILSON IN 1919. JAPAN JOINED IN SUPPORTING THE DECLARATION AS WELL.

SAN REMO CONFERENCE

ON APRIL 25, 1920, THE SUPREME COUNCIL OF THE ALLIED POWERS REACHED AN AGREEMENT DURING THE SAN REMO CONFERENCE TO ASSIGN BRITAIN WITH THE RESPONSIBILITY OF OVERSEEING PALESTINE. ADDITIONALLY, THEY DECIDED TO

IMPLEMENT THE BALFOUR DECLARATION AS OUTLINED IN ARTICLE TWO OF THE MANDATE. SUBSEQUENTLY, ON JULY 24, 1922, THE LEAGUE OF NATIONS APPROVED THE MANDATE PROJECT, WHICH OFFICIALLY CAME INTO EFFECT ON SEPTEMBER 29, 1923.

FOLLOWING THE ESTABLISHMENT OF THE MANDATE OVER PALESTINE, BRITISH ASSISTANCE FACILITATED THE PURCHASE OF PALESTINIAN LANDS BY JEWISH IMMIGRANTS. BY THE BEGINNING OF 1929, THE NUMBER OF IMMIGRANTS WHO HAD ENTERED PALESTINE UNDER BRITISH OCCUPATION SURPASSED ONE HUNDRED THOUSAND. FURTHERMORE, THERE WERE THOUSANDS OF ILLEGAL INFILTRATORS. THIS INFLUX OF IMMIGRATION COINCIDED WITH THE SEIZURE OF LAND FROM ARAB FARMERS, RESULTING IN THEIR EXPULSION FROM THEIR OWN TERRITORIES.

ESTABLISHMENT OF THE STATE OF ISRAEL

ON MAY 14, 1948, THE OFFICIAL ANNOUNCEMENT OF THE ESTABLISHMENT OF THE STATE OF ISRAEL WAS MADE, WITHOUT SPECIFYING ITS EXACT BORDERS. FIVE ARAB NATIONS, ALONG WITH THE ARAB POPULATION, ENGAGED IN WARFARE

AGAINST THE NEWLY FORMED NATION. FOLLOWING THE 1948 CONFLICT, JERUSALEM WAS DIVIDED INTO TWO SECTIONS: THE WESTERN PART, WHICH FELL UNDER ISRAELI CONTROL, AND THE EASTERN PART, WHICH CAME UNDER JORDANIAN JURISDICTION. IN NOVEMBER OF THE SAME YEAR, A BUFFER ZONE WAS CREATED BETWEEN THE TWO PARTS, LEADING TO AN INFORMAL DELINEATION OF BORDERS BETWEEN THE CONFLICTING PARTIES. THIS DELINEATION WAS TAKEN INTO ACCOUNT DURING THE SIGNING OF THE ARMISTICE AGREEMENT IN 1949 BETWEEN ISRAEL AND LEBANON, EGYPT, JORDAN, AND SYRIA, WHEREBY THESE NATIONS AGREED TO A CEASEFIRE.

THE PALESTINE LIBERATION ORGANIZATION

ON DECEMBER 3, 1948, THE ISRAELI PRIME MINISTER, DAVID BEN-GURION, MADE AN ANNOUNCEMENT STATING THAT WEST JERUSALEM WOULD SERVE AS THE CAPITAL OF THE NEWLY FORMED ISRAELI STATE. IN 1950, JORDAN OFFICIALLY DECLARED ITS SOVEREIGNTY OVER EAST JERUSALEM.

THE FIRST SESSION OF THE PALESTINIAN NATIONAL COUNCIL TOOK PLACE IN EAST JERUSALEM ON MAY 29, 1964, DURING WHICH AN ORGANIZATION CALLED THE PALESTINIAN LIBERATION WAS ESTABLISHED.

IN 1967, FOLLOWING A SETBACK, ISRAEL TOOK CONTROL OF EAST JERUSALEM, WHICH WAS PREVIOUSLY UNDER JORDANIAN AUTHORITY, AND CONSIDERED IT AN INTEGRAL PART OF THEIR TERRITORY. HOWEVER, THE INTERNATIONAL COMMUNITY, FOR THE MOST PART, DID NOT RECOGNIZE THIS ANNEXATION AND STILL REGARDS EAST JERUSALEM AS A DISPUTED AREA. THEY ADVOCATE FOR RESOLVING THIS ISSUE THROUGH PEACEFUL NEGOTIATIONS. AS A RESULT, MOST FOREIGN EMBASSIES AND CONSULATES ARE LOCATED IN TEL AVIV AND ITS SUBURBS, WHILE ISRAELI GOVERNMENT DEPARTMENTS ARE PRIMARILY SITUATED IN WEST JERUSALEM.

THIS INCLUDES THE PARLIAMENT, PRIME MINISTER'S OFFICE, PRESIDENT'S OFFICE, AND THE SUPREME COURT. IN A HOSTILE ACT IN 1969, MICHAEL DENNIS ROHN, A JEWISH AUSTRALIAN CITIZEN, WAS RESPONSIBLE FOR THE BURNING OF AL-AQSA MOSQUE.

UNRAVELING THE FORGOTTEN CHAPTERS: ORIGINS OF THE PALESTINIAN CAUSE

IN 1967, WHEN ISRAELI FORCES TOOK CONTROL OF EAST JERUSALEM, THE KNESSET PASSED A RESOLUTION ON JUNE 27TH TO ANNEX ARAB JERUSALEM TO ISRAEL BOTH POLITICALLY AND ADMINISTRATIVELY, BASED ON ORDER NO. 2064. SUBSEQUENTLY, THE ISRAELI GOVERNMENT ISSUED "LAW AND ORDER ORDER" NO. 1 OF 1967, WHICH BROUGHT THE AREA UNDER ISRAELI LAWS AND ADMINISTRATIVE SYSTEMS.

ON JULY 30TH, 1980, THE ISRAELI KNESSET APPROVED THE "UNIFIED JERUSALEM" BASIC LAW, DECLARING THAT JERUSALEM, WITH ITS TWO PARTS, WOULD BE RECOGNIZED AS THE UNIFIED CAPITAL OF ISRAEL AND THE SEAT OF THE STATE'S PRESIDENCY, GOVERNMENT, KNESSET, AND SUPREME COURT. CONSEQUENTLY, PALESTINIAN AUTHORITY LAWS NO LONGER APPLIED TO EAST JERUSALEM, WHICH HAD ALSO SERVED AS THE CENTER OF THE PALESTINIAN JERUSALEM GOVERNORATE. ISRAEL VIEWED THE PRESENCE OF PALESTINIANS IN EAST JERUSALEM AS AN IMPEDIMENT TO ITS EFFORTS TO UNIFY THE CITY. ITS OBJECTIVE WAS TO ERODE THE IDENTITY OF JERUSALEM'S INHABITANTS AND FULLY INTEGRATE THEM INTO ISRAEL'S ECONOMIC AND SOCIAL SYSTEM.

THIS INVOLVED TARGETING PALESTINIAN INSTITUTIONS, CIVIL SOCIETY ORGANIZATIONS, AND SOCIAL INITIATIVES IN ORDER TO EXERT CONTROL OVER AL-AQSA MOSQUE AND JERUSALEM, WITH THE AIM OF ALTERING THE CITY'S ARAB AND ISLAMIC CHARACTER AND REPLACING IT WITH A JEWISH IDENTITY. BEFORE THIS ISRAELI ENDEAVOR, THERE WERE NUMEROUS PREVIOUS ATTEMPTS TO ESTABLISH JERUSALEM AS THE CAPITAL, AS ISRAEL HAD LONG CONSIDERED "TEL AVIV" AS A TEMPORARY CAPITAL WHILE ANTICIPATING THE ANNEXATION OF JERUSALEM. HOWEVER, MOST COUNTRIES DID NOT TAKE THIS DECISION SERIOUSLY, RESULTING IN EMBASSIES REMAINING IN TEL AVIV OR REFUSING TO RELOCATE. THE SECURITY COUNCIL REJECTED ANY ISRAELI EFFORTS IN THIS REGARD.

UNTIL THE TRUMP ADMINISTARTION HAD DECLARED JERUSALEM AS THE CAPITAL OF ISRAEL AGAINST MERE OBJECTIONS FROM ARAB STATES.

THE OSLO ACCORDS

Signed in 1993, marked a significant political shift as the Palestinians and Israelis agreed to discuss the fate of Jerusalem at the negotiation table. This peace agreement, signed in Washington, D.C. on September 13, 1993, was named after the Norwegian city of Oslo where the secret talks leading to the agreement took place.

According to the agreement, a Palestinian transitional self-government authority (later known as the Palestinian National Authority) and an elected legislative council would be established for the Palestinian people in the West Bank and Gaza Strip. This arrangement would last for a maximum of five years in exchange for the PLO's recognition of Israel. The agreement also outlined that during these transitional years, negotiations between the two sides would occur with the goal of achieving a permanent settlement based on Security Council Resolutions 242 and 338.

THESE NEGOTIATIONS WOULD ADDRESS THE REMAINING ISSUES AT HAND.

LONG BEFORE THE CURRENT CONFLICT ERUPTED ON THE 7TH OF OCTOBER, 2023, THE OCCUPATION FORCES CONTINUED TO ENGAGE IN VIOLATIONS AGAINST THE PALESTINIAN PEOPLE, DISREGARDING INTERNATIONAL LAW. PALESTINE HAS ALWAYS FACED CHALLENGING CIRCUMSTANCES AND SERIOUS OBSTACLES DUE TO THE ISRAELI OCCUPATION AND AGGRESSIVE ACTIONS AGAINST ITS PEOPLE, LAND, HOLY SITES, AND RIGHTS.

THE CURRENT WAR IS BUT AN OUTCOME OF A NEW GENERATION OF PALESTINIANS, I KNOW THEM AS THE CHILDREN OF STONES, THE GENERATIONS THAT FOUGHT BACK THE INJUSTICE WITH NOTHING BUT A SLING-SHOT AND A STONE, THEY HAVE RISEN UP, RAISING THE FLAG OF RESISTANCE AND ASSERTING THEIR RIGHT TO SELF-DETERMINATION. THEIR RIGHT CAN NO LONGER BE IGNORED.

DECODING RUSSIA'S STANCE: INTERPRETING THEIR POSITION ON THE WAR BETWEEN ISRAEL AND PALESTINIAN FACTIONS

IN THE WAKE OF THE RECENT CLASHES BETWEEN PALESTINIAN RESISTANCE AND ISRAELI FORCES, ALONG WITH THE RESULTING CASUALTIES, DEVASTATION, AND RECIPROCAL BOMBINGS IN THE OCCUPIED PALESTINIAN TERRITORIES, RUSSIAN PRESIDENT VLADIMIR PUTIN HAS OFFERED THE FIRST RUSSIAN RESPONSE. PUTIN POINTED OUT THAT THIS CRISIS IS A DIRECT CONSEQUENCE OF THE FAILURE OF AMERICAN POLICIES IN THE REGION. HE EMPHASIZED THAT THE ONLY VIABLE SOLUTION TO RESOLVE THIS CRISIS IS BY ADHERING TO THE UNITED NATIONS SECURITY COUNCIL RESOLUTION CONCERNING THE CREATION OF AN INDEPENDENT PALESTINIAN STATE. FURTHERMORE, HE CALLED UPON BOTH CONFLICTING PARTIES TO MINIMIZE HARM TO CIVILIANS. MEANWHILE, UKRAINIAN PRESIDENT VOLODYMYR ZELENSKY HAS EXPRESSED CONCERN THAT THE CONFLICT IN THE GAZA STRIP BETWEEN ISRAEL AND HAMAS COULD POTENTIALLY DISTRACT THE INTERNATIONAL COMMUNITY FROM WHAT HE REFERS TO AS THE "RUSSIAN INVASION" OF UKRAINE. HE ACCUSES

SUPPORT TO PALESTINIAN MOVEMENTS, A CLAIM THAT RUSSIA DENIES.

RUSSIAN POSITION ON THE PALESTINIAN-ISRAELI CONFLICT

THE RUSSIAN STANCE ON THE PALESTINIAN-ISRAELI CONFLICT IS INFLUENCED BY SEVERAL KEY FACTORS AND DETERMINANTS. THESE INCLUDE RUSSIA'S GEOPOLITICAL INTERESTS IN THE MIDDLE EAST AND ITS ASPIRATION TO REGAIN ITS HISTORICAL ROLE AS A REGIONAL POWER. FURTHERMORE, RUSSIA HAS STRONG HISTORICAL AND CULTURAL TIES WITH NUMEROUS ARAB NATIONS, WHICH ALSO IMPACT ITS POSITION. ANOTHER CONTRIBUTING FACTOR IS THE SIGNIFICANT PRESENCE OF AN ARAB MINORITY WITHIN RUSSIA, INFLUENCING ITS FOREIGN POLICIES. ADDITIONALLY, RUSSIA'S STANCE ON OTHER INTERNATIONAL MATTERS SUCH AS THE SYRIAN CRISIS AND THE IRANIAN NUCLEAR ISSUE ALSO PLAY A ROLE.

THE RUSSIAN STANCE IS ALSO SHAPED BY THE GEOPOLITICAL RIVALRY WITH THE UNITED STATES, WHICH BACKS ISRAEL. CONVERSELY, RUSSIA HAS BEEN STRENGTHENING ITS ECONOMIC AND TRADE TIES WITH ISRAEL. THESE VARIOUS FACTORS CONTRIBUTE TO RUSSIA'S SPECIFIC STANCE ON THE PALESTINIAN ISSUE AND THE CONFLICT BETWEEN PALESTINIAN FACTIONS AND ISRAEL. RUSSIA STRIVES TO MAINTAIN A RELATIVE NEUTRALITY IN ORDER TO ENHANCE ITS INFLUENCE AS A MEDIATOR BETWEEN THE PARTIES INVOLVED. CONSEQUENTLY, IT CAN BE OBSERVED THAT THE HISTORICAL RUSSIAN POSITION ON THE ARAB-ISRAELI CONFLICT IS INFLUENCED BY SEVERAL FACTORS. RUSSIA PERCEIVES ITSELF AS A NEUTRAL NATION IN THIS CONFLICT AND DOES NOT FULLY ALIGN WITH EITHER SIDE. IT AIMS TO ACT AS A MEDIATOR BETWEEN THE CONFLICTING PARTIES IN ORDER TO FACILITATE A PEACEFUL RESOLUTION OF THE CONFLICT.

DECODING RUSSIA'S STANCE: INTERPRETING THEIR POSITION ON THE WAR BETWEEN ISRAEL AND PALESTINIAN FACTIONS

RUSSIA CONSISTENTLY ADVOCATES FOR A SOLUTION INVOLVING TWO STATES IN ACCORDANCE WITH RESOLUTIONS OF INTERNATIONAL LEGITIMACY. IT MAINTAINS SIGNIFICANT DIPLOMATIC AND ECONOMIC TIES WITH BOTH ISRAEL AND ARAB COUNTRIES. RUSSIA ALSO OPPOSES UNILATERAL ISRAELI DECISIONS AND ACTIONS SUCH AS SETTLEMENTS, WHILE ACCUSING THE UNITED STATES OF BIAS TOWARDS ISRAEL AND A LACK OF NEUTRALITY.

THIS INDICATES THAT THE RUSSIAN STANCE IS ADAPTABLE AND INFLUENCED BY MOSCOW'S GEOPOLITICAL INTERESTS IN THE REGION. IN RELATION TO THE ONGOING CONFLICT BETWEEN PALESTINIANS AND ISRAELIS, RUSSIAN FOREIGN MINISTER SERGEI LAVROV HAS URGED ALL INVOLVED PARTIES TO INTENSIFY THEIR EFFORTS, CREATING FAVORABLE CONDITIONS FOR A SWIFT RESUMPTION OF NEGOTIATIONS BETWEEN PALESTINIANS AND ISRAELIS. THE ULTIMATE GOAL OF THESE NEGOTIATIONS SHOULD BE THE ESTABLISHMENT OF AN INDEPENDENT PALESTINIAN STATE WITHIN THE TERRITORIES, FOSTERING PEACEFUL COEXISTENCE BETWEEN THE TWO STATES.

A GOLDEN OPPORTUNITY..

IN A TIME WHEN THE ONGOING RUSSIAN-UKRAINIAN WAR SHOWS NO SIGNS OF ENDING AFTER ALMOST A YEAR AND A HALF, WITH WESTERN AND AMERICAN SUPPORT FOR UKRAINE AGAINST RUSSIA, RUSSIA MAY VIEW THE CURRENT CRISIS BETWEEN ISRAELIS AND PALESTINIANS AS A VALUABLE OPPORTUNITY. WITH THE WEST AND THE UNITED STATES HEAVILY INVOLVED IN SUPPORTING ISRAEL, RUSSIA MIGHT SEEK TO EXPLOIT THIS SITUATION IN VARIOUS WAYS.

ONE POSSIBLE TACTIC IS TO SHIFT BLAME ONTO THE UNITED STATES. THE RUSSIAN PRESIDENT HAS ALREADY CLAIMED THAT THE ESCALATING CONFLICT BETWEEN ISRAELIS AND PALESTINIANS IS A CLEAR EXAMPLE OF AMERICAN POLICY FAILURE IN THE REGION. HE ACCUSES WASHINGTON OF NOT ACTIVELY PURSUING COMPROMISE SOLUTIONS THAT WOULD BENEFIT BOTH SIDES OF THE CONFLICT, INSTEAD EXERTING PRESSURE ON THE PALESTINIANS WHILE IGNORING THEIR BASIC INTERESTS. RATHER THAN CALLING FOR AN END TO HOSTILITIES, THE WEST AND THE UNITED STATES HAVE CHOSEN TO SUPPORT ISRAEL.

DECODING RUSSIA'S STANCE: INTERPRETING THEIR POSITION ON THE WAR BETWEEN ISRAEL AND PALESTINIAN FACTIONS

RUSSIA ALSO CRITICIZES THE UNITED STATES FOR MONOPOLIZING MEDIATION EFFORTS AND REDIRECTING THE DIALOGUE BETWEEN PALESTINIANS AND ISRAELIS AWAY FROM A POLITICAL RESOLUTION AND THE ESTABLISHMENT OF AN AUTONOMOUS AND INDEPENDENT PALESTINIAN STATE. RUSSIA MAINTAINS THAT THE RESOLUTION TO THE PALESTINIAN ISSUE SHOULD ALIGN WITH THE TWO-STATE PRINCIPLE, IN ACCORDANCE WITH SECURITY COUNCIL AND UNITED NATIONS RESOLUTIONS, WHILE ALSO RESPECTING THE RIGHTS OF THE PALESTINIAN PEOPLE.

THE ESCALATION OF RUSSIAN ASSAULTS ON UKRAINE MAY BE FACILITATED BY RUSSIA CAPITALIZING ON THE GLOBAL FOCUS ON EVENTS UNFOLDING IN THE PALESTINIAN TERRITORIES. THIS SERVES AS A REFLECTION OF RUSSIA'S STRATEGIC APPROACH TO UTILIZING DIVERSIONARY TACTICS TO BOLSTER ITS INTERNATIONAL STANDING AND PURSUE ITS STRATEGIC OBJECTIVES. UKRAINIAN PRESIDENT VOLODYMYR ZELENSKY HAS HIGHLIGHTED THIS MATTER, ACCUSING RUSSIA OF BACKING PALESTINIAN RESISTANCE MOVEMENTS AS A MEANS TO "DIVERT ATTENTION"

FROM WHAT HE PERCEIVES AS A "RUSSIAN INVASION" OF HIS COUNTRY. HE EXPRESSED HIS CONCERN THAT THE WORLD MIGHT FOCUS ON THE EVENTS IN PALESTINE AND OVERLOOK THE SITUATION IN UKRAINE.

FINALLY, ALTHOUGH THE ARAB WORLD WOULD LIKE TO SEE AN IMPARTIAL SIDE MEDIATING THE CONFLICT, IT SEEMS UNLIKELY SO, GIVEN THE SPEED BY WHICH THE UNITED STATES HAVE REACTED TO THE CONFLICT, HOWEVER, THE RUSSIANS WOULD SEIZE THE OPPORTUNITY TO MEDIATE IF ASKED TO DO SO. SEEMINGLY, THE ONLY SIDE THAT WOULD WOULD BE ABLE TO MEDIATE ON THE CONFLICT AND SHOW IMPARTIALITY, ARE THE EGYPTIANS, AND THE JORDANIANS, AND THE ARAB GULD STATES LED BY SAUDI ARABIA, AND THAT MAY SOUND AS A WEAKER SIDE AS OPPOSED TO THE RUSSIANS, GIVEN THE ARABS AND THE EGYPTIANS CONTROVERSIAL BUT SADLY ESSTENTIAL RELATIONS WITH THE US, BUT THIS SIDE COULD PLAY A MORE STRONGER ROLE, FIRST OF ALL, THE EGYPTIANS ARE NEXT TO GAZA, CONTROLLING THE BORDERLINE, AND THEIR INSISTANCE

NOT TO ALLOW A LAND INVASION OF ISRAELI FORCES INTO GAZA, WHICH WILL CAUSE A HUGE HUMANITARIAN CRISIS, AND A HUGE INFLUX OF REFUGES INTO SINAI, CAN BE CONSIDERED AS A GOOD HAND IN THE PALESTINIAN SIDE, SECONDLY, THE ARAB GULF CONTROL THE OIL, WHICH IS A WEAPON THAT CAN BE USED VERY EFFECTIVELY, IF THINGS GO SOUTH, THESE POINTS AMONG OTHERS, MAKE THE EGYPTIAN AND ARAB GULF STATES SIDE A MORE STRONGER AND RELIABLE THAN THE RUSSIAN ONE.

AFTERMATH OF THE 'AL-AQSA FLOOD' OPERATION ON ISRAEL'S ECONOMY

THE AL-QASSAM BRIGADES, THE MILITANT ARM OF THE HAMAS MOVEMENT, DECLARED THAT THEY HAVE LAUNCHED APPROXIMATELY 5,000 ROCKETS TOWARDS ISRAEL DURING OPERATION "AL-AQSA FLOOD," WHILE ISRAEL RETALIATED WITH OPERATION IRON SWORDS, COMMENCING FOUR HOURS AFTER THE PALESTINIAN ASSAULT. THE INCREASE IN SECURITY INCIDENTS ON THE THIRD DAY OF OPERATIONS WILL FURTHER EXACERBATE ISRAEL'S ECONOMIC CHALLENGES, WHICH HAVE BEEN COMPOUNDED BY SOCIAL PROTESTS AND POLITICAL UNREST TRIGGERED BY THE JUDICIAL REFORM LAW. THESE FACTORS HAVE NEGATIVELY IMPACTED EXPECTATIONS OF ECONOMIC GROWTH, INFLATION RATES, EXCHANGE RATES, AND ISRAEL'S CREDIT RATING. IN THIS ARTICLE, WE WILL EXPLORE THE POTENTIAL CONSEQUENCES OF OPERATION "AL-AQSA FLOOD" ON THE ISRAELI ECONOMY.

AFTERMATH OF THE 'AL-AQSA FLOOD' OPERATION ON ISRAEL'S ECONOMY

THE DEVALUATION OF THE ISRAELI CURRENCY: CURRENCY MARKETS EXHIBIT RAPID REACTIONS TO SECURITY AND GEOPOLITICAL CRISES, WITH THE ISRAELI SHEKEL SWIFTLY DEPRECIATING AGAINST THE DOLLAR TO ITS LOWEST POINT IN NEARLY SEVEN YEARS. ON OCTOBER 9, 2023, THE EXCHANGE RATE STOOD AT APPROXIMATELY 3.92 SHEKELS PER DOLLAR, COMPARED TO THE PRE-OPERATION RATE OF 3.86 SHEKELS PER DOLLAR ON OCTOBER 6. THIS SIGNIFIES A DECLINE OF ROUGHLY 2%.

THE SHEKEL IS EXPECTED TO CONTINUE DECLINING AGAINST THE DOLLAR AND OTHER FOREIGN CURRENCIES, WHICH WILL LIKELY RESULT IN HIGHER PRICES FOR IMPORTED GOODS IN THE NEAR FUTURE. THIS, IN TURN, WILL FURTHER EXACERBATE THE ALREADY HIGH INFLATION RATE, WHICH STOOD AT 5.3% IN 2022 – THE HIGHEST IT HAS BEEN SINCE OCTOBER 2008. IN RESPONSE TO THE RISING INFLATION, THE ISRAELI CENTRAL BANK MAY OPT TO RAISE THE INTEREST RATE AT ITS UPCOMING MEETING ON OCTOBER 23RD. THE LAST INTEREST RATE HIKE OCCURRED IN MAY WHEN IT WAS INCREASED FROM 4.5% TO 4.75%. SUBSEQUENTLY, THE RATE WAS KEPT STABLE IN

AFTERMATH OF THE 'AL-AQSA FLOOD' OPERATION ON ISRAEL'S ECONOMY

IN THE JULY AND SEPTEMBER 2023 MEETINGS.

THE TEL AVIV STOCK EXCHANGE EXPERIENCED A SIGNIFICANT DROP IN ITS INDICES, WITH LOSSES EXCEEDING 6% FOLLOWING A 4% DECLINE AT THE OPENING YESTERDAY, SUNDAY. ADDITIONALLY, GOVERNMENT BOND PRICES FELL BY UP TO 3% IN THE AFTERMATH OF THE ATTACK. THE MAIN STOCK INDEX, TA-35, HAS NOW RECORDED A DECREASE OF ABOUT 7.5%, REACHING 1694 POINTS. THESE LOSSES ARE THE LARGEST SEEN IN OVER THREE YEARS.

THE CENTRAL BANK OF ISRAEL HAS ANNOUNCED ITS INTENTION TO SELL FOREIGN CURRENCIES FOR THE VERY FIRST TIME IN ITS HISTORY. THIS MOVE IS AIMED AT PROVIDING LOCAL BANKS WITH DOLLAR LIQUIDITY AS PART OF AN UNPRECEDENTED PROGRAM TO SUPPORT THE MARKETS. IN A STATEMENT ISSUED ON MONDAY, THE BANK OF ISRAEL REVEALED PLANS TO SELL UP TO $30 BILLION AND INTERVENE IN THE MARKET IN THE NEAR FUTURE TO STABILIZE FLUCTUATIONS IN THE SHEKEL EXCHANGE RATE AND

ENSURE SUFFICIENT LIQUIDITY. THIS MARKS THE CENTRAL BANK'S FIRST INTERVENTION IN THE MARKETS IN APPROXIMATELY TWO YEARS AND THE FIRST INSTANCE OF SELLING US DOLLARS FROM ITS CASH RESERVES.

DETERIORATING ECONOMIC CRISES: OVER THE RECENT MONTHS, CREDIT RATING AGENCIES HAVE ISSUED WARNINGS ABOUT THE POTENTIAL DOWNGRADE OF ISRAEL'S CREDIT RATING AND FUTURE ECONOMIC PROSPECTS. THESE CONCERNS STEM FROM THE IMPACT OF JUDICIAL REFORM ON THE COUNTRY'S ECONOMIC GROWTH. IT WAS ANTICIPATED THAT ISRAELI ECONOMIC GROWTH WOULD DECLINE FROM 6.5% IN 2022 TO 1.5% IN 2023. IN APRIL, MOODY'S REVISED ITS OUTLOOK FOR ISRAEL FROM "POSITIVE" TO "STABLE" DUE TO WIDESPREAD PROTESTS AGAINST THE GOVERNMENT'S JUDICIAL REFORM PLANS. THE OPPOSITION VIEWS THESE PLANS AS AN ATTEMPT TO DIMINISH THE JUDICIARY'S AUTHORITY IN FAVOR OF THE EXECUTIVE BRANCH. A CREDIT RATING DOWNGRADE WOULD RESULT IN HIGHER DEBT SERVICE COSTS FOR ISRAEL.

THE TOURISM INDUSTRY: THE SECTOR IS LIKELY TO FACE A PERIOD OF INSTABILITY AS A NUMBER OF AIRLINES HAVE RECENTLY CANCELED MULTIPLE FLIGHTS TO TEL AVIV. AMONG THE COMPANIES THAT HAVE HALTED THEIR FLIGHTS TO BEN GURION AIRPORT IN TEL AVIV ARE LUFTHANSA, EMIRATES AIRLINES, RAINAIR, AEGEAN AIRLINES, AND AIR FRANCE. THIS HAS RESULTED IN HOTELS RECEIVING NUMEROUS CALLS TO THEIR SERVICE CENTERS AND WITNESSING AN INCREASE IN CANCELLATIONS FOR FUTURE RESERVATIONS BY TOURISTS. THE REPERCUSSIONS OF THESE DEVELOPMENTS MAY HAVE A SIGNIFICANT IMPACT ON ISRAEL'S TOURISM REVENUES, WHICH CURRENTLY CONTRIBUTE APPROXIMATELY 2.8% TO THE COUNTRY'S GDP AND ACCOUNT FOR AROUND 3.5% OF TOTAL EMPLOYMENT.

FOREIGN DIRECT INVESTMENTS: THEY ARE LIKELY TO EXPERIENCE A NOTABLE DECREASE FOLLOWING THE "AL-AQSA FLOOD" CAMPAIGN, WHICH SAW A SIGNIFICANT DROP IN THE FIRST QUARTER OF 2023, REACHING 60% COMPARED TO THE AVERAGE OF THE FIRST QUARTERS IN BOTH 2020 AND 2022.

AFTERMATH OF THE 'AL-AQSA FLOOD' OPERATION ON ISRAEL'S ECONOMY

IT SHOULD BE HIGHLIGHTED THAT THE ESTIMATED VALUE OF FOREIGN INVESTMENTS IN ISRAEL WAS AROUND $28 BILLION IN 2022.

THE EXORBITANT PRICE OF CONFLICT: THE ISRAELI ECONOMY SUFFERS IMMENSE FINANCIAL RAMIFICATIONS DUE TO WAR, AMOUNTING TO BILLIONS OF SHEKELS. THESE COSTS ARE TWOFOLD – THE DIRECT EXPENSES INCURRED BY THE ISRAELI ARMY AND SECURITY SERVICES, ENCOMPASSING EXPENDITURES ON AMMUNITION AND LOGISTICAL EQUIPMENT, AND THE INDIRECT COSTS MANIFESTED THROUGH THE CLOSURE OF BUSINESSES AND THE DETRIMENTAL IMPACT ON TOURISM, TRADE, AND OTHER SECTORS. THE ECONOMIC BURDENS ARISING FROM THE ONGOING MILITARY OPERATION MAY FURTHER INTENSIFY THE POLITICAL PRESSURE ON THE CURRENT "NETANYAHU" GOVERNMENT, WHICH ALREADY GRAPPLES WITH INTERNAL CHALLENGES. THE ISRAELI PEOPLE PERCEIVE A LACK OF FOCUS ON TRADITIONAL EXTERNAL THREATS DUE TO THE GOVERNMENT'S PREOCCUPATION WITH POLITICAL DISPUTES.

CLOSURE OF GAS FIELDS: CHEVRON HAS BEEN INSTRUCTED BY ISRAEL TO HALT NATURAL GAS PRODUCTION AT THE "TAMAR" PLATFORM DUE TO SAFETY CONCERNS. THIS DECISION MAY RESULT IN A DECREASE IN SHIPMENTS OR EVEN A DELAY, PARTICULARLY AS EGYPT PLANS TO RESUME LNG EXPORTS THIS YEAR, JUST BEFORE THE ONSET OF THE EUROPEAN WINTER. THE "TAMAR" OFFSHORE FIELD, SITUATED 24 KILOMETERS WEST OF ASHKELON IN THE NORTHERN GAZA STRIP, HAS BEEN SUBJECTED TO REPEATED MISSILE ATTACKS BY PALESTINIAN FACTIONS. GAS IS EXTRACTED FROM SIX WELLS IN THE FIELD, EACH WITH A DAILY PRODUCTION CAPACITY RANGING FROM 7.1 TO 8.5 MILLION CUBIC METERS.

FINALLY, IT SHOULD BE NOTED THAT THOSE NUMBERS AND FACTS GOBACK TO THE BGEINNINGS OF THE CONFLICT, EXACTLY, OCT 15, 2023

AL-AQSA FLOOD: ASSESSING IRAN'S ROLE - OPPORTUNITY OR THREAT

DESPITE THE POTENTIAL GAINS THAT IRAN MAY SEEM TO ACHIEVE, EVEN IF SOME OF THEM ARE NOTICEABLE, FROM THE RECENT EVENTS FOLLOWING THE LAUNCH OF OPERATION "AL-AQSA FLOOD" BY THE PALESTINIAN RESISTANCE FACTIONS ON OCTOBER 7TH, THE CURRENT DEVELOPMENTS AND THE INTRICATE INTERNATIONAL CALCULATIONS SURROUNDING IRAN'S DEALINGS, COUPLED WITH THE POSSIBILITY OF FURTHER ESCALATION IN THE REGION AND THE POTENTIAL EXPANSION OF THE WAR, INDICATE THAT IRAN FINDS ITSELF IN AN UNFAVORABLE POSITION. THIS IS SUPPORTED BY VARIOUS FACTUAL EVIDENCE, INCLUDING THE IRANIAN POLITICIANS' ATTEMPTS TO DISASSOCIATE THEMSELVES FROM ANY CONNECTION BETWEEN THE ACTIONS OF THE PALESTINIAN FACTIONS AND IRAN'S SUPPORT.

AL-AQSA FLOOD: ASSESSING IRAN'S ROLE - OPPORTUNITY OR THREAT

HOW DID IRAN DEAL WITH THE "AL-AQSA FLOOD"?

EVER SINCE THE COMMENCEMENT OF THE "AL-AQSA FLOOD" MISSIONS ON OCTOBER 7TH, A SIGNIFICANT NUMBER OF IRANIANS HAVE CONGREGATED IN NUMEROUS PROVINCES ACROSS THE EAST, WEST, NORTH, AND SOUTH TO DEMONSTRATE THEIR BACKING AND JOY FOR THESE OPERATIONS. THE GATHERED INDIVIDUALS HAVE CHANTED SLOGANS IN SUPPORT NOT ONLY OF THE MISSIONS THEMSELVES BUT ALSO IN HONOR OF SUPREME LEADER ALI KHAMENEI AND THE LATE QUDS FORCE COMMANDER, QASEM SOLEIMANI, WHO WAS KILLED IN A US AIRSTRIKE NEAR BAGHDAD INTERNATIONAL AIRPORT ON JANUARY 3, 2020. THESE GATHERINGS APPEARED TO BE A SWIFT RESPONSE TO THE "AL-AQSA FLOOD," BUT IN SOME WAY, THEY SERVED AS A MEANS OF BOLSTERING THE POLITICAL REGIME IN TEHRAN. NOT ONLY WERE THEY SHOWING THEIR SUPPORT FOR THE SUPREME LEADER, BUT THEY WERE ALSO INDIRECTLY ENDORSING IRANIAN FOREIGN POLICY IN THE REGION. THIS INCLUDED BACKING VARIOUS FACTIONS IN THE AREA, INCLUDING PALESTINIAN FACTIONS,

A STANCE THAT HAS FACED CRITICISM FROM CERTAIN SEGMENTS OF THE IRANIAN POPULATION AND CERTAIN POLITICIANS.

ON THAT SAME DAY, IRAN OFFICIALLY DECLARED ITS ENDORSEMENT OF THE OPERATION. GENERAL YAHYA RAHIM SAFAVI, ADVISOR TO SUPREME LEADER ALI KHAMENEI FOR MILITARY AFFAIRS, AND PRESIDENT EBRAHIM RAISI BOTH EXPRESSED THEIR SUPPORT. RAISI WENT ON TO STATE THAT "THE SITUATION HAS CHANGED." DURING A SPEECH ON OCTOBER 10, THE FOURTH DAY OF THE OPERATIONS, IRANIAN LEADER KHAMENEI ECHOED THIS SENTIMENT WHILE ATTENDING A GRADUATION CEREMONY FOR MILITARY OFFICERS AT IMAM ALI MILITARY UNIVERSITY IN TEHRAN. IT IS WORTH NOTING THAT WHEN IRANIAN OFFICIALS MENTION THEIR COUNTRY'S SUPPORT FOR THE OPERATION, THEY ARE NOT REFERRING TO LOGISTICAL OR MATERIAL ASSISTANCE, BUT RATHER MORAL SUPPORT AND ACCEPTANCE.

ISRAELI AND WESTERN ACCUSATIONS AGAINST IRAN OF "STANDING BEHIND THE OPERATION"

ALTHOUGH THERE WERE NO IRANIAN MILITARY OFFICERS OR SOLDIERS INVOLVED IN THE "AL-AQSA FLOOD" OPERATIONS, IRAN HAS BEEN ACCUSED OF SUPPORTING OR BEING BEHIND THE OPERATION. THE ISRAELI AMBASSADOR TO BERLIN, RON PROSOR, ACCUSED IRAN OF BEING RESPONSIBLE FOR THE MAJOR ATTACK LAUNCHED BY HAMAS ON ISRAEL. HE STATED THAT THOSE RESPONSIBLE FOR THE ATTACK WILL BE PUNISHED AND THAT EVERYTHING WILL BE DONE TO DEFEND AND PUNISH THEM. PROSOR ALSO CLAIMED THAT IRAN IS BEHIND THIS AND WILL TRY TO ESCALATE THE SITUATION INTO A STATE OF WAR. THESE STATEMENTS BY THE ISRAELI AMBASSADOR IN BERLIN ALIGN WITH REPORTS FROM WITHIN ISRAEL THAT ACCUSE TEHRAN OF SUPPORTING THE OPERATION.

IN REGARDS TO THE WEST, WHILE THE ACCUSATIONS WERE NOT OFFICIALLY MADE, PROMINENT WESTERN NEWSPAPERS AND MEDIA OUTLETS ALLEGED THAT IRAN WAS INVOLVED IN SUPPORTING THE OPERATION. ON OCTOBER 10, US NATIONAL SECURITY ADVISOR JACK SULLIVAN STATED THAT IRAN HAD A BROAD INVOLVEMENT IN THE HAMAS ATTACK, BUT THERE WAS NO SPECIFIC INFORMATION INDICATING THAT TEHRAN HAD OFFERED EXPLICIT SUPPORT FOR THE UNPRECEDENTED ATTACK. SULLIVAN ADDED THAT IRAN PLAYED A SIGNIFICANT ROLE IN SUPPORTING THE MILITARY WING OF HAMAS, PROVIDING TRAINING, CAPABILITIES, SUPPORT, AND MAINTAINING COMMUNICATION WITH HAMAS FOR MANY YEARS.

IT IS IMPORTANT TO NOTE THAT SULLIVAN USED THE TERM "SUPPORT IN THE BROAD SENSE" TO EMPHASIZE IRAN'S GENERAL SUPPORT FOR ARMED FACTIONS IN THE REGION, INCLUDING PALESTINIAN FACTIONS. THE WASHINGTON POST ALSO REPORTED, BASED ON INFORMATION FROM WESTERN AND MIDDLE EASTERN SECURITY OFFICIALS, THAT THE ATTACK ON ISRAEL HAD BEEN PLANNED A YEAR AGO WITH FOUNDATIONAL SUPPORT FROM

THE ISLAMIC REPUBLIC, WHICH INVOLVED MILITARY TRAINING, FINANCIAL AND LOGISTICAL AID.

ACCORDING TO A REPORT BY THE WALL STREET JOURNAL, IT WAS REVEALED THAT THE PLANNING FOR THE HAMAS OPERATION OCCURRED DURING A MEETING HELD IN BEIRUT IN AUGUST. THE MEETING INVOLVED LEADERS OF HAMAS, HEZBOLLAH, AND REPRESENTATIVES OF ARMED GROUPS, WHO MET WITH OFFICERS FROM THE REVOLUTIONARY GUARD. ISMAIL QAANI, THE COMMANDER OF THE QUDS FORCE, BEGAN COORDINATING EXTENSIVELY WITH PALESTINIAN FACTIONS AND HEZBOLLAH SINCE APRIL.

ALTHOUGH HAMAS CONFIRMED ITS INVOLVEMENT IN THE ATTACKS AS A DECISION MADE BY PALESTINIANS, THERE WAS NO MENTION OF IRAN'S SUPPORT. THE REPORT CONCLUDED BY STATING THAT ISRAELI SECURITY OFFICIALS HAVE THREATENED TO ATTACK IRAN IF ITS INVOLVEMENT IN THE ATTACK IS PROVEN.

TEHRAN'S NUCLEAR PROGRAM AND THE "AL-AQSA FLOOD": OPPORTUNITY OR THREAT?

IRAN HAS ALREADY EXPERIENCED INDIRECT ADVANTAGES FOLLOWING THE COMMENCEMENT OF THE "AL-AQSA FLOOD" OPERATIONS A FEW DAYS AGO. ONE OF THE MOST SIGNIFICANT GAINS IS THE IMPACT ON ISRAELI SECURITY AND THE MILITARY BALANCE BETWEEN IRAN AND ISRAEL. THE MEDIA IN IRAN CONTINUES TO EMPHASIZE THIS POINT, HIGHLIGHTING THE SHIFT IN MILITARY AND SECURITY DYNAMICS BETWEEN THE TWO COUNTRIES IN VARIOUS REGIONS, NOT JUST LIMITED TO THE MIDDLE EAST. THIS SHIFT FAVORS IRAN, EVEN IF ONLY TEMPORARILY.

IN ADDITION TO THESE SECURITY AND MILITARY CONSIDERATIONS, THE IRANIAN POLITICAL REGIME HAS ALSO REAPED POLITICAL BENEFITS FROM THESE OPERATIONS. IT HAS USED THEM TO BOLSTER ITS REGIONAL "POWER AND INFLUENCE," WHICH HAS HAD A POSITIVE IMPACT INTERNALLY AS WELL. ESSENTIALLY, THE WAR IN GAZA HAS GIVEN THE POLITICAL REGIME IN TEHRAN GREATER SIGNIFICANCE AND VITALITY WITHIN ITS OWN BORDERS.

However, it is evident from the current situation in the Israeli-Palestinian conflict that these reciprocal actions have the potential to evolve into a situation where Iran may face a threat.

Western and Israeli Accusations Against Iran of "Involvement" in the Gaza War Alongside "Hamas"

The Western and Israeli claims against Iran regarding their alleged support or involvement in the "Al-Aqsa Flood" operations, alongside Palestinian factions, particularly Hamas, may serve as a pretext for targeting significant Iranian assets. This could include locations both within and outside of Iran. Israel has formally accused Iran, and American intelligence is currently seeking more information on the matter. Israel and certain influential nations desire such a scenario to justify striking Iranian facilities, be it domestic or foreign. These targets could consist of missile or drone production sites, and potentially even some nuclear installations,

SHOULD THE PALESTINIAN-ISRAELI ESCALATION EVOLVE INTO A LARGER REGIONAL CONFRONTATION. CONSEQUENTLY, ATTACKING VALUABLE IRANIAN TARGETS WOULD BE SEEN AS LEGITIMATE AND POSSIBLY ACCEPTABLE ON THE INTERNATIONAL STAGE.

THE REGIONAL EXPANSION OF THE WAR AND HEZBOLLAH

EVER SINCE THE COMMENCEMENT OF THE GAZA WAR A FEW DAYS AGO, IRANIAN OFFICIALS HAVE CONSISTENTLY EMPHASIZED THAT THEIR COUNTRY HAS NO INVOLVEMENT OR CONNECTION TO THESE ATTACKS. THESE ASSURANCES HAVE COME FROM THE HIGHEST-RANKING OFFICIALS IN TEHRAN AND CONTINUE TO BE REITERATED. THIS CAN BE ATTRIBUTED TO IRAN'S UNDERSTANDING OF THE POTENTIAL CHALLENGES AND THREATS IT MAY FACE IF IT WERE TO ADMIT TO "SUPPORTING OR BEING BEHIND" THE AL-AQSA FLOOD OPERATIONS.

However, it is worth considering that Iran may become entangled in the ongoing escalation between Palestine and Israel, if factions loyal to Iran join the frontlines. For instance, Hezbollah, which issued a statement on October 9, two days after the conflict began, stated that three of its members were killed in an Israeli airstrike in southern Lebanon. This came after the Israeli army announced the identification of "a number of launching operations from Lebanese territory towards us." Hezbollah clarified that "groups of the Islamic Resistance" launched guided missiles at Israel, targeting the Pranit barracks and the Avivim barracks of the Israeli army in response to the Israeli attack on Lebanese towns.

PRIOR TO THAT, FACTIONS IN IRAQ THAT ARE LOYAL TO IRAN AND SEVERAL OTHER GROUPS IN THE AREA HAVE RELEASED STATEMENTS SUGGESTING THAT THEY MAY CARRY OUT ATTACKS ON AMERICAN TARGETS IN THE REGION IF THE UNITED STATES SUPPORTS ISRAEL AGAINST HAMAS. THESE GROUPS AND FACTIONS CONTINUE TO ISSUE NUMEROUS WARNINGS AND STATEMENTS REGARDING THIS MATTER.

THESE PIECES OF INFORMATION INDICATE THAT THERE IS STILL A POSSIBILITY OF PRO-IRANIAN GROUPS IN THE REGION, ALONG WITH IRAN ITSELF, GETTING INVOLVED IN THE ONGOING PALESTINIAN-ISRAELI CONFLICT, WHICH IS CURRENTLY REFERRED TO AS THE "AL-AQSA FLOOD." THIS POSSIBILITY REMAINS ON THE TABLE AND IS CLOSE AT HAND, PARTICULARLY IN LIGHT OF THE UNITED STATES' DEPLOYMENT OF ITS MILITARY FORCES IN THE EASTERN MEDITERRANEAN. HOWEVER, SO FAR, IT APPEARS THAT THIS DEPLOYMENT IS AN ATTEMPT TO DETER THESE GROUPS FROM TAKING ACTION AGAINST ISRAEL OR EVEN AGAINST AMERICAN INTERESTS IN THE REGION.

IRAN'S BACKED MILITIA AND THE UNITED STATES' POSSIBLE ENTRY INTO THE WAR

THE RECENT ESCALATION BETWEEN PALESTINE AND ISRAEL HAS TAKEN A MORE SIGNIFICANT TURN THAN IN THE PAST. IT IS GRADUALLY CASTING A SHADOW OVER THE REGION AND IS ATTRACTING ATTENTION FROM MAJOR COUNTRIES ON THE INTERNATIONAL STAGE. THE UNITED STATES HAS DISPATCHED AN UNPRECEDENTED NUMBER OF MILITARY FORCES AND EQUIPMENT TO ISRAEL. THIS COULD SUGGEST THAT WASHINGTON AIMS TO "DETER" IRAN AND ITS PROXY ALLIES FROM ENGAGING IN A LARGER CONFLICT WITH ISRAEL. HOWEVER, IT COULD ALSO INDICATE THAT THE CONFLICT IS INTENSIFYING AND THAT A CLASH BETWEEN IRANIAN-BACKED GROUPS AND ISRAEL WILL PROMPT A RESPONSE FROM THE UNITED STATES.

SINAI'S SINISTER SCHEME: UNVEILING THE THREATS OF LAND LIQUIDATION AND FORCED DISPLACEMENT OF PALESTINIANS

EGYPT HAS BEEN AMASSING AID FROM BOTH INTERNATIONAL AID GROUPS AND MIDDLE EASTERN NATIONS IN NORTHERN SINAI, WITH THE INTENTION OF SENDING THEM INTO GAZA AS SOON AS THE RAFAH CROSSING IS OPENED. ADDITIONALLY, PRESIDENT ABDEL FATAH EL-SISI COMMANDED THE COUNTRY TO INITIATE A BLOOD DRIVE ON THURSDAY.

AT A MILITARY SCHOOL SPEECH ON THURSDAY NIGHT, PRESIDENT SISI DECLARED EGYPT'S WILLINGNESS TO COOPERATE WITH EVERYBODY, EMPHASIZING THEIR EAGERNESS TO SEND HUMANITARIAN AND MEDICAL ASSISTANCE TO THE GAZA STRIP. HE UNDERSCORED THE NATION'S ROLE AS A STEADFAST COMMUNICATOR BETWEEN ISRAEL AND PALESTINIAN FACTIONS.

THE WAR BETWEEN ISRAEL AND GAZA HAS BEEN A SOURCE OF INTERNATIONAL TENSIONS. THE CONFLICT HAS BEEN LONG-STANDING, WITH LITTLE PROGRESS BEING MADE TOWARDS A RESOLUTION. THE VIOLENCE AND DESTRUCTION RESULTING FROM THE WAR HAS HAD A DEVASTATING IMPACT ON GAZA, AND ITS INHABITANTS.

THE WHOLE POPULATION OF THE NORTHERN GAZA STRIP HAS BEEN INSTRUCTED TO EVACUATE BY ISRAEL. ON SATURDAY, ISRAELI PRIME MINISTER BENJAMIN NETANYAHU DEMANDED THAT PALESTINIANS IN GAZA LEAVE THE AREA IMMEDIATELY. AMIDST THE DROPPING OF BOMBS, GAZANS ARE LEFT WITHOUT A PLACE TO FLEE TO.

EVENTHOUGH, EGYPTIAN AND MULTIPLE STATES HAVE BEEN TRYING TO SEND AID TO THE GAZA STRIP, THE PASSAGEWAY AT THE BORDER OF GAZA HAS BEEN INOPERABLE DUE TO THE DESTRUCTION OF THE INFRASTRUCTURE CAUSED BY ISRAELI AIRSTRIKES.

AS THE ALREADY DESPERATE SITUATION IN GAZA BECOMES <u>INCREASINGLY DIRE BY THE HOUR</u>, THE DEMAND FOR A HUMANITARIAN CORRIDOR TO PROVIDE FOOD, WATER, FUEL AND MEDICAL SUPPLIES GROWS LOUDER. ISRAEL'S DECISION TO EVACUATE THE 1.1 MILLION PEOPLE OF GAZA CITY ON FRIDAY HAS FURTHER HEIGHTENED THE PRESSURE.

THE SINISTER SCHEME TO END THE DREAM OF LIBERATION..

ON TUESDAY, EGYPTIAN SECURITY PERSONNEL, WHO WERE UNNAMED, INFORMED SKY NEWS ARABIA THAT ISRAEL FORMULATED A PLAN TO ELIMINATE PALESTINIAN LAND AND COERCE PALESTINIANS TO OPT FOR EITHER DEATH OR ABANDONING THEIR HOMES. THE WILLINGNESS OF MANY PALESTINIANS TO MIGRATE TO EGYPT, DESPITE THE RISKS, IS NOT CERTAIN.

FOR PALESTINIANS, THE DISPLACEMENT THAT OCCURRED DURING THE FOUNDATION OF THE STATE OF ISRAEL IN 1948 -- REFERRED TO AS THE NAKBA, WHICH TRANSLATES TO "CATASTROPHE" IN ARABIC -- HAS BEEN A CONTINUOUS SOURCE OF INTERGENERATIONAL TRAUMA.

IN FACT, 70 PERCENT OF GAZANS ARE REFUGEES WHO WERE EITHER FORCED TO LEAVE OR HAD TO FLEE FROM PARTS OF THE LAND THAT IS NOW ISRAEL AND WERE NEVER ALLOWED TO COME BACK.

HOWEVER, THE DISPLACEMENT OF PALESTINIANS TO SINAI WILL WITHOUT A DOUBT END THE PALESTINIAN HOPES FOR A STATE OF THEIR OWN, IT WOULD COMPELTELY ELIMINATE THE PROPOSAL OF THE TWO-STATE SOLUTION. EGYPT KNOWS THAT, THE ISRAELIS KNOW THAT, AND THE PALESTINIANS KNOW THAT.

ISMAIL HANIYEH, CHAIRMAN OF THE POLITICAL BUREAU OF HAMAS, DECLARED SATURDAY THAT: "THERE WILL BE NO MIGRATION FROM THE WEST BANK OR GAZA, NOR FROM GAZA TO EGYPT, AND I SALUTE THE BROTHERS IN EGYPT."

"I SAY TO MY BROTHERS IN EGYPT THAT WE INTEND TO REMAIN IN OUR LAND, AND YOUR POSITION IS THE SAME AS OUR OWN."

OTHER REASONS EXIST....

EGYPT IS FACED WITH A DECADES-LONG DILEMMA WITH REGARDS TO ALLOWING A LARGE NUMBER OF PALESTINIANS TO LEAVE GAZA. SECURITY IS AN ISSUE OF CONCERN FOR CAIRO, AND IT DESIRES TO PREVENT ANY IMPRESSION OF BEING INVOLVED WITH A MOVEMENT THAT COULD FORCE PALESTINIANS TO LEAVE OF GAZA, AND PALESTINE FOREVER.

AS TIMOTHY KALDAS, DEPUTY DIRECTOR OF THE TAHRIR INSTITUTE FOR MIDDLE EAST POLICY BASED IN WASHINGTON D.C. STATED, "FROM A POLITICAL POINT OF VIEW, NO ARAB COUNTRY WISHES TO BE PERCEIVED AS AIDING IN THE UPROOTING OF THE PALESTINIAN POPULATION."

EGYPT HAS ACCEPTED A SUBSTANTIAL AMOUNT OF REFUGEES FROM OTHER CONFLICTS, INCLUDING THOSE WHO HAD TO EVACUATE DUE TO THE ARMED CONFLICT IN SUDAN. NEVERTHELESS, THE SITUATION IN SINAI IS DELICATE AND THE PALESTINIAN MATTER IS SIGNIFICANTLY MORE COMPLICATED.

ANALYSTS STATED THAT THE INFLUX OF A LARGE AMOUNT OF PALESTINIAN REFUGEES INTO EGYPT WOULD POSE CONSIDERABLE POLITICAL AND SAFETY DANGERS. PUBLIC SENTIMENT IS WONDERFULLY SUPPORTIVE TO THE PALESTINIAN CAUSE, HOWEVER THE PUBLIC IS ALSO WEARY OF THE RISKS INVOLVED IN ALLOWING LARGE AMOUNT OF REFUGEES INTO EGYPT.

EGYPTIANS ARE THOUGHT TO BE VERY CONCERNED WITH THE ISSUE OF NATIONAL SECURITY, AS IT WOULD BE HARD TO STOP HAMAS COMBATANTS FROM INFILTRATING THE COUNTRY AMONGST THE REFUGEE POPULATION. THEY MAY BE WORRIED THAT WEAPONS COULD BE SMUGGLED IN AS WELL, AND THE FEAR THAT IT MAY USED TO ATTACK ISRAEL FROM EGYPTIAN LANDS, AS HAMAS HAS DONE THROUGH LEBANON, WHICH COULD CAUSE SERIOUS CONFLICT BETWEEN ISRAEL AND EGYPT.

PRESIDENT SISI HAS VOICED HIS BACKING FOR A TWO-STATE RESOLUTION IN THE ISRAELI-PALESTINIAN CRISIS, EMPHASIZING HIS WISH FOR PEACE.

FURTHERMORE, HE REFUSED ANY ATTEMPTS BY MULTIPLE ENTITIES TO PASS A RESOLUTION THAT DIVERGES FROM THE 1993 OSLO ACCORDS, THE GLOBAL COMPACTS THAT WERE DESIGNED TO CREATE A PALESTINIAN STATE.
HE STATED THAT THE PLIGHT OF THE PALESTINIANS IS AN ISSUE THAT CONCERNS ALL ARABS, AND THAT THEY SHOULD REMAIN STEADFAST ON THEIR NATIVE SOIL.

THE NAQAB DESERT: A HISTORY OF FAILED ISRAELI DREAMS

EGYPTIAN PRESIDENT ABDEL FATTAH AL-SISI'S MENTION OF THE "NAQAB DESERT" AS A POTENTIAL RELOCATION SITE FOR PALESTINIANS FROM GAZA UNTIL ISRAEL CEASES ITS OPERATIONS HAS ONCE AGAIN BROUGHT ATTENTION TO THIS REGION. THE NAQAB DESERT HAS LONG BEEN CONSIDERED AS A POTENTIAL DESTINATION FOR DISPLACING PALESTINIANS FROM THE WEST BANK AND GAZA STRIP, OFTEN UNDER THE GUISE OF "LAND EXCHANGE" PROJECTS. HOWEVER, EXPERTS IN ISRAELI AFFAIRS, INTERVIEWED BY ASHARQ AL-AWSAT, NOTE THAT THIS PROPOSAL HAS BEEN CONSISTENTLY REJECTED.

DURING A PRESS CONFERENCE WHERE HE RECEIVED THE GERMAN CHANCELLOR, OLAF SCHULZ, THE EGYPTIAN PRESIDENT ISSUED A WARNING ABOUT THE ONGOING MILITARY OPERATIONS IN THE GAZA STRIP. HE EXPRESSED CONCERN OVER THE POTENTIAL "SECURITY AND MILITARY REPERCUSSIONS" THAT COULD ARISE AND ESCALATE BEYOND CONTROL. THE PRESIDENT FURTHER MENTIONED THAT IF PALESTINIANS WERE DISPLACED TO SINAI,

IT WOULD EFFECTIVELY TRANSFER THE CONFLICT TO THAT REGION, MAKING IT A BASE FOR ATTACKING ISRAEL. HE EMPHASIZED THAT THIS DISPLACEMENT WOULD NOT BE LIMITED TO GAZA BUT COULD EXTEND TO THE WEST BANK, WITH PALESTINIANS POTENTIALLY BEING RELOCATED TO JORDAN UNTIL ISRAEL CONCLUDES ITS OPERATION IN GAZA.

COMMON BORDERS..

THE NAQAB DESERT SPANS ACROSS THE SOUTHERN PARTS OF THE PALESTINIAN TERRITORIES UNDER OCCUPATION, COVERING AN AREA OF OVER 14 THOUSAND SQUARE KILOMETERS. IT IS BORDERED BY JORDAN TO THE EAST AND THE SINAI DESERT TO THE WEST. TO THE SOUTH, IT IS SEPARATED FROM THE RED SEA BY THE CITY OF EILAT, WHILE THE CITY OF HEBRON (LOCATED SOUTH OF THE WEST BANK) IS ONE OF THE CLOSEST PALESTINIAN CITIES TO ITS NORTHERN SIDE.

DESPITE THE VAST EXPANSE OF THIS AREA, THE POPULATION IS RELATIVELY SMALL AND DOES NOT SURPASS, AS ESTIMATED BY PALESTINIANS, "100,000 RESIDENTS LIVING IN APPROXIMATELY 46 VILLAGES." OUT OF THESE VILLAGES, 36 ARE NOT RECOGNIZED BY THE OCCUPYING AUTHORITIES, AND THEIR POPULATIONS RANGE FROM A MINIMUM OF 400 TO A MAXIMUM OF 5,000. ACCORDING TO REPORTS FROM PALESTINIAN MEDIA, THE ARAB COMMUNITIES IN THE NAQAB DESERT "EXPERIENCE EVIDENT NEGLECT FROM THE ISRAELI OCCUPATION AUTHORITIES," EVEN THOUGH CERTAIN SETTLEMENTS AND MILITARY PROJECTS HAVE BEEN ESTABLISHED IN LIMITED PARTS OF THE REGION, MOST NOTABLY THE DIMONA NUCLEAR REACTOR.

A POOR REGION...

ACCORDING TO DR. SAEED OKASHA, AN EXPERT IN ISRAELI AFFAIRS AT THE AL-AHRAM CENTER FOR POLITICAL AND STRATEGIC STUDIES, THE NAQAB DESERT REGION IS CHARACTERIZED BY ITS LACK OF RESOURCES AND THE HIGH COST ASSOCIATED WITH ITS DEVELOPMENT. THIS IS ONE OF THE MAIN REASONS WHY ISRAEL REPEATEDLY EXPRESSES A DESIRE TO DISPOSE OF THE NAQAB DESERT IN ORDER TO ACQUIRE MORE ADVANTAGEOUS LAND FOR SETTLEMENT PROJECTS OR TO FACILITATE THE DISPLACEMENT OF PALESTINIANS TO NEIGHBORING COUNTRIES. SOURCES HAVE CLARIFIED TO ASHARQ AL-AWSAT THAT THE PROPOSAL FOR THE NAQAB DESERT IS PART OF A LONG-STANDING CONCEPT OF EXCHANGING TERRITORIES WITH NEIGHBORING COUNTRIES OR THE PALESTINIAN AUTHORITY. THIS IDEA HAS BEEN ON THE TABLE SINCE THE 1950S. IT WAS FIRST PRESENTED TO FORMER EGYPTIAN PRESIDENT GAMAL ABDEL NASSER,

WHO REJECTED IT. THE PROPOSITION RESURFACED IN 2000 WHEN IT WAS OFFERED TO THE LATE PALESTINIAN PRESIDENT YASSER ARAFAT. IN EXCHANGE FOR RELINQUISHING 600 SQUARE KILOMETERS OF WEST BANK LAND TO ACCOMMODATE ISRAELI SETTLEMENTS, ARAFAT ALSO DECLINED . THE ISRAELI SECURITY PERSPECTIVE IS CONCERNED ABOUT THE ESTABLISHMENT OF NEW PALESTINIAN COMMUNITIES ALONG ITS BORDERS.

A PLAN NOT SO NEW....A PLAN BEING RENEWED...

IN EARLY 2010, GIORA EILAND, THE FORMER ISRAELI NATIONAL SECURITY ADVISOR, PUBLISHED A STUDY SUGGESTING THAT THE NEW KINGDOM OF JORDAN COULD SERVE AS THE HOMELAND FOR PALESTINIANS. ACCORDING TO EILAND, THIS PROPOSED KINGDOM WOULD CONSIST OF THREE REGIONS: THE WEST BANK, THE EAST BANK, AND GREATER GAZA, WHICH WOULD INCORPORATE A PORTION OF EGYPT.

Ahmed Aboul Gheit, the Secretary-General of the League of Arab States and former Minister of Foreign Affairs of Egypt (2004-2011), discussed the incident of Israel's land exchange proposal in his memoirs titled "My Testimony," published in 2012. The proposal involved Egypt allocating land in Sinai to the Palestinians in exchange for Israel relinquishing land in the Naqab Desert to Egypt.

According to Aboul Gheit's memoirs, he noted that these suggestions had been previously presented to former Egyptian President Anwar Sadat and were later reintroduced to former President Hosni Mubarak. However, Mubarak strongly rejected the proposal and cautioned his officials to be cautious and avoid falling into the trap.

THE BELIEF OF SULEIMAN GOUDA, AN EGYPTIAN WRITER AND POLITICAL ANALYST, IS THAT THE ISRAELIS' CONSTANT SENSE OF LIMITED STRATEGIC DEPTH IN THEIR TERRITORY IS THE DRIVING FORCE BEHIND THEIR CONTINUAL PURSUIT OF EXPANSION WHENEVER THE OPPORTUNITY ARISES AND THE MEANS ARE AVAILABLE. THIS HAS BEEN MANIFESTED THROUGH WARS LIKE THE ONE IN 1967, AS WELL AS THROUGH PROPOSALS FOR LAND EXCHANGES OR THE DISPLACEMENT OF PALESTINIANS TO EGYPT AND JORDAN ON MULTIPLE OCCASIONS.

OTHER SOURCES HAVE EMPHASIZED THOUGH, THAT THE DISPLACEMENT PROJECTS HAVE BEEN UNDER CONSIDERATION FOR A LONG TIME, BUT LAND EXCHANGE PROJECTS HAVE NOT BEEN TAKEN SERIOUSLY. THE ULTIMATE GOAL FOR ISRAEL HAS ALWAYS BEEN TO DISPLACE THE PALESTINIANS TO NEIGHBORING COUNTRIES, UNDER THE UMBRELLA THAT THEY ARE TRYING TO ALLEVIATE THE BURDENS OF THE PALESTINIANS. AS RIDICULAS AS THAT MAY SOUND.

FURTHERMORE, THIS OBJECTIVE HAS CONSISTENTLY FACED REJECTION FROM EGYPT AND JORDAN DURING THE CURRENT CRISIS, AS WELL AS FROM THE INTERNATIONAL COMMUNITY AT LARGE, EXCEPT FOR INTERMITTENT AND VARIED SUPPORT FROM THE UNITED STATES. IT IS BELIEVED THAT THE PROJECT HAS BEING REINTRODUCED AS A "TEST BALLOON," TO TEST THE REACTION OF THE EGYPTIANS AND JORDANIANS, BUT AFTER THE EGYPTIAN PRESIDENT'S PRESS CONFERENCE, IT APPEARS THAT THOSE PLANS WILL NOT PROGRESS BEYOND HOPES AND DREAMS, AND "ISRAEL AND THE UNITED STATES HAVE RECEIVED A DECISIVE OFFICIAL AND POPULAR RESPONSE FROM EGYPT."

GLOBAL CATASTROPHE: ASSESSING THE THREAT OF WORLD WAR 3 IN THE MIDDLE EAST

No one anticipated it, but the Israeli-Palestinian conflict has been brought back to the forefront of global attention in an intense manner. Despite efforts for diplomatic initiatives through out the years. They were all short-lived. The false sense of peace that had been achieved was merely a 'calm before the storm.' The recent conflict has destroyed the artificial harmony the region appeared to be in.

The current situation is still not well understood, it is not but a reaction to the years of injustice faced by the Palestinians for the last 30-40 years of occupation, the constant provocation by the Israelis throughout the years has finally drawn the last straw!

OCTOBER 6TH... A DATE WITH HUGE SIGNIFICANCE TO THE ARAB WORLD

OCTOBER 6TH MARKED NEARLY HALF A CENTURY SINCE THE YOM KIPPUR WAR, AND IN THE SAME VEIN, ISRAEL WAS MET WITH ANOTHER SURPRISE ATTACK, THIS TIME COMING FROM HAMAS. THIS ORGANISATION LAUNCHED AN UNPRECEDENTED ATTACK ON THE SOUTHERN PARTS OF THE COUNTRY. AT TIMES, HAMAS FIGHTERS HAD CONTROL OVER WHOLE TOWNS, SOMETHING THAT WAS ONLY SEEN IN MOVIES AND SERIES.

IT WAS A DISASTER FOR THE ISRAELI SECRET SERVICE, WHICH WAS NOT AWARE OF ANY MAJOR OFFENSIVE THAT HAD BEEN PLANNED FOR MONTHS OR MAYBE YEARS. THEY DID NOT BELIEVE THAT HAMAS WOULD GO BEYOND THE FRAMEWORK OF CONTROLLED HOSTILITIES AND START A FULL-SCALE WAR. THIS MEANS THAT BOTH PARTIES ARE NOW ENTERING AN UNKNOWN TERRITORY IN THE DISPUTE, WHICH INCREASES THE RISK OF A MAJOR ESCALATION AND EVEN A WAR BEYOND GAZA, A LARGE FULL SCALE WAR.

NETANYAHU'S FALIURE..

THE RECENT CONFLICT IS A CLEAR FAILURE FOR BENJAMIN NETANYAHU, ISRAEL'S PRIME MINISTER, WHO IS NOW HAVING TO ACT AS A WARLORD IN THE MIDDLE OF THE NATION'S MOST SIGNIFICANT INTERNAL POLITICAL DISCORD. ACCORDING TO NETANYAHU, THE SOLUTION TO THE PALESTINIAN-ISRAELI CONFLICT WAS NEVER THE TWO-STATE SOLUTION WHICH HIS RIGHT-WING NATIONALIST GOVERNMENT HAD EVEN STOPPED MENTIONING. RATHER, IT WAS TO MAINTAIN THE CURRENT STATE OF OCCUPATION AND OPPRESSION OF THE PALESTINIANS, WHICH SOME OF THE WORLD'S TOP HUMAN RIGHTS ORGANISATIONS ARE IDENTIFYING AS 'APARTHEID'.

NETANYAHU'S PLAN BEFORE THE RECENT CONFLICT WAS TO LINK INTERNATIONAL NORMALISATION OF RELATIONS WITH THE ARAB COUNTRIES, WHICH BEGAN WITH THE ABRAHAM ACCORDS AND WAS TO CULMINATE IN A DEAL WITH SAUDI ARABIA, WITH DOWNPLAYING THE 'PALESTINE QUESTION'.

THIS IS NOW LOOKING INCREASINGLY UNLIKELY; NOT ONLY DUE TO THE PALESTINIANS' REFUSAL TO BE 'MANAGED', BUT THE GRUESOME IMAGES OF THE BOMBING IN GAZA ARE LIKELY TO HINDER ANY PROGRESS. IT IS ALSO WORTH MENTIONING THAT THE ARAB POPULATION STILL SHOWS STRONG SOLIDARITY WITH PALESTINE.

THE LAND INVASION OF GAZA

THE ISRAELI ARMY, WHICH IS EQUIPPED WITH THE MOST MODERN MILITARY EQUIPMENT COULD SUFFER AN IMMENSE MILITARY DISASTER IF THEY INITIATE AN ATTACK ON THE DENSELY POPULATED GAZA STRIP. THIS AREA IS OCCUPIED BY A DETERMINED GROUP THAT IS DETERMINED TO FIGHT TO THE DEATH AND KNOWS THE TERRITORY INSIDE OUT.

WITH A POPULATION OF TWO AND A HALF MILLION PEOPLE, A LARGE PROPORTION OF WHOM ARE CHILDREN, NETANYAHU'S DEMAND THAT THEY SHOULD LEAVE IS PARTICULARLY FOOLISH, CONSIDERING THERE IS NO WAY FOR THEM TO ESCAPE TO SAFETY. A HUMANITARIAN DISASTER IS UNAVOIDABLE.

HEZBOLLAH, THE SYRIAN MILITIA, IRAN, RUSSIA, AND EGYPT ALL PART OF THE EQUATION???

THE CONSEQUENCES OF THE CURRENT SITUATION COULD BE DIRE FOR ISRAEL, AS IT COULD FACE WAR ON MULTIPLE FRONTS. SPECULATION HAS INCREASED ABOUT HOW MUCH IRAN WAS AWARE OF THE PLANS LEADING UP TO THE CRISIS.

A SCENARIO AKIN WORSE TO ISRAEL THAN THE "YOM KIPPUR WAR" WILL BE POSSIBLE IF HEZBOLLAH LAUNCHES SIMULTANEOUS ATTACKS ON THE NORTHERN FRONT. UNDENIABLY, HEZBOLLAH HAS A HEFTY ARSENAL, AND THE POSSIBILITY OF THE LEBANESE MILITIA JOINING THE CONFLICT IN GAZA, TRANSFORMING IT FROM A LIMITED CONFLICT TO A MUCH LARGER REGIONAL ENGAGEMENT, IS THE MOST PIVOTAL FACTOR OF THE CURRENT CRISIS. IN TERMS OF MILITARY MIGHT, HEZBOLLAH IS VASTLY SUPERIOR TO HAMAS, BOASTING AN ARSENAL OF OVER TEN TIMES THE AMOUNT OF ROCKETS. AS SOON AS THE GROUND OFFENSIVE IN GAZA KICKS OFF, THE DEMAND FOR ASSISTANCE TO THEIR PALESTINIAN 'SIBLINGS' WILL SURGE DRAMATICALLY.

FURTHERMORE, IF ISRAEL INTENDS TO EMPLOY GROUND TROOPS IN LEBANON AND CONFRONT HEZBOLLAH ON THE GROUND, AS THEY HAVE DECLARED IN REGARDS TO HAMAS, THERE IS A CHANCE THE WAR COULD EVENTUALLY GROW TO INCLUDE IRAN. IT IS IMPROBABLE THE ISLAMIC REPUBLIC WOULD REMAIN STILL AND WITNESS

THEIR MOST PRIZED RESOURCE BE DESTROYED. INVADING LEBANON WILL WIDEN THE CONFLICT TO SYRIA (WITH NUMEROUS IRANIAN AND PRO-IRANIAN MILITIAS PRESENT).

EGYPT, IS ALSO A HUGE QUESTION MARK, THE EGYPTIAN PRESIDENT HAS ASSERTED NUMEROUS TIMES THAT IT WILL NOT ALLOW THE INFLUX OF PALESTINIAN REFUGEES TO SINAI, MEANING IT WILL NOT ALLOW A LAND INVASION OF GAZA (WHICH WILL CAUSE THE INFLUX), SO HOW WILL EGYPT RESPOND TO THE LAND INVASION IS A SERIOUS MATTER, WE ARE TALKING ABOUT ONE OF THE MOST MODERNIZED ARMIES IN THE REGION AND THE WORLD. AND IF EGYPT IS DIRECTLY INVOLVED IN THE WAR, WE CAN EXPECT THE ARAB GULF STATES TO SUPPORT THEIR ALLY EXTENSIVELY, NOT ONLY THROUGH FINANCING THE EGYPTIAN DEFENSIVE, BUT ALSO THROUGH APPLYING INTERNATIONAL PRESSURE ON THE UNITED STATES AD ISRAEL, POSSIBLY THROUGH AN EMBARGO OF OIL TO THE WEST, IT HAS BEEN DONE BEFORE IN 1973.

RUSSIA, ON THE OTHER HAND, COULD ENJOY AN ADVANTAGE IN THIS CONFLICT, THEY MIGHT BE GRANTED A REPRIEVE IN UKRAINE DUE TO THE DISTRACTED WEST. ALSO, MOSCOW MAY DIRECTLY BACK AN IRAN-HAMAS-HEZBOLLAH UNION.

CHINA ON THE OTHER HAND , HAS DEPLOYED 6 WARSHIPS TO THE MIDDLE EAST REGION., ON OCT 22, 2023, AND CHINA IS FORMALLY ALLIED TO RUSSIA.

WITH THE CURRENT INVOLVMENT OF THE **UNITED STATES**, BY SENDING AIR CARRIERS TO THE REGION, THIS PALESTINIAN- ISRAELI CONFLICT COULD EASILY SPIRAL TO A LARGER FULL SCALE WAR, THAT CAN ONLY BE ACKNOWLEDGED AS A WORLD WAR 3, IF ALL THE ABOVE SCENARIOS TAKE PLACE.

Animals and Cockroaches.... How Israel Echoes the Rawandan Genocide

"We are fighting against human animals". This is how Israeli defence minister Yoav Gallant described what he called a "complete siege" on Gaza, following a surprise attack by Hamas on Israel.

Since the start of the Palestinain-Israeli conflict that started on Oct, 7th, Israel has insisted on making plans for an invasion of Gaza to so call "eradicate" Hamas. It is essential to remind prime minister Benjamin Netanyahu and his associates that this is an endeavor that will not be successful.

Hamas was formed because of the forceful taking over of Palestinian lands by Jewish settlers and the confining of Palestinians in separate lands similar to the Bantustans of apartheid South Africa. Israel can eliminate Hamas as an organization but will never be able to eradicate the Palestinian resistance. If by any chance Hamas is demolished,

ANOTHER PALESTINIAN ORGANIZATION WILL RISE FROM ITS ASHES. MORE LIKELY, THE NEW ORGANIZATION WILL BE MORE RADICAL AND VIOLENT.

AN OFFENSIVE INCURSION INTO GAZA WILL NEVER PUT AN END TO THIS CONFLICT, ONLY FUEL IT. THE ONLY ANSWER IS TO PERMIT PALESTINIANS AND JEWS TO LIVE TOGETHER IN A TWO STATE SOLUTION.

ISRAEL ASSERTS THAT IT IS LOOKING FOR SAFETY, BUT IT DOES SO BY SEIZING PALESTINIAN PROPERTIES AND CONTINUALLY SUBJECTING THEM TO VARIOUS FORMS OF HUMILIATION. THIS APPROACH HAS CAUSED IT TO LAND IN A DEPLORABLE STATE: THE FORMATION OF AN APARTHEID SYSTEM AND THE ENDLESS BRUTALISATION AND DEHUMANISATION OF PALESTINIANS.

ISRAEL AND RWANDA…

IT WAS THE EUROPEANS THAT HELPED FORMED ISRAEL, AND UNFORTUNETLY THE EUROPEAN CONCEPT OF MODERNITY HAS CAUSED TURMOIL IN MANY REGIONS, INCLUDING RWANDA. DURING THE COLONIAL PERIOD, EUROPEANS EMPLOYED TUTSIS TO LEAD A GOVERNMENT THAT MISTREATED HUTUS.

HOWEVER, WHEN MOVING TOWARDS INDEPENDENCE, THE EUROPEANS ASSISTED IN THE "LIBERATION" OF HUTUS IN 1957. THE HUTU "REVOLUTION" WAS PLANNED TO END THE DOMINATION OF HUTUS BY TUTSIS, BUT THE RESULT WAS A DOMINATION OF TUTSIS BY HUTUS. THIS WAS DONE THROUGH ETHNIC CLEANSING OF TUTSIS, WHICH INCLUDED MASS MURDER AND THE EXILE OF HUNDREDS OF THOUSANDS OF TUTSIS.

ONCE IN CONTROL, HUTU SUPREMACISTS CREATED AN APARTHEID STATE IN WHICH TUTSIS WERE VIEWED AS LOWER CLASS CITIZENS. THEY WERE RESTRICTED FROM MANY RIGHTS DUE TO THE STATE-IMPOSED QUOTAS. CONSEQUENTLY, HUTU POWER RECREATED THE VERY ETHNIC DOMINATION THEY BLAMED THE TUTSI FOR HAVING CONTROLLED.

ISRAEL USES THIS HUTU SCRIPT. JEWISH AUTHORITY IS EXERCISED THROUGH THE SEGREGATION OF PALESTINIANS. THIS IS MOST OBVIOUS IN GAZA AND THE WEST BANK. THERE, PALESTINIANS REGULATED BY AN APARTHEID SYSTEM HAVE NO PRIVILEGES WHATSOEVER. WHEN THE HUTU APARTHEID STATE WAS CHALLENGED BY THE TUTSI-LED RPF, HUTU SUPREMACISTS SOUGHT

A DEFINITIVE SOLUTION TO ANNIHILATE EVERY TUTSI OR SEND THEM INTO EXILE.

ONE CAN DETECT HINTS OF THIS WHEN ISRAEL LEADERS USE BARELY CLEAR WORDS REGARDING INVADING GAZA TO PURIFY IT OF HAMAS. OF COURSE, THEY ARE NOT DISCUSSING HAMAS BUT RATHER CLEANSING THAT AREA OF PALESTINIANS.

IN THE SPRING OF 1994, RWANDA WAS THE SITE OF AN UNPRECEDENTED ATROCITY WHEN ONE MILLION PEOPLE WERE BRUTALLY SLAUGHTERED. THE KILLING WAS INDISCRIMINATE AND EVEN INCLUDED FAMILY MEMBERS, FELLOW CONGREGANTS, AND STUDENTS. IT WAS ONLY WHEN THE RPF ARMY DEFEATED THE HUTU SUPREMACISTS THAT THE MASSACRE FINALLY ENDED. THE AFTERMATH OF THE GENOCIDE WAS ONE OF THE LARGEST QUESTIONS: COULD THE HUTU AND TUTSI COEXIST PEACEFULLY?

CURRENTLY, RWANDA IS ONE OF THE MOST PEACEFUL NATIONS IN AFRICA, A STARK CONTRAST TO THE MID-1990S, WHEN NUMEROUS ACADEMICS AND "EXPERTS" ASSERTED THAT HUTUS AND TUTSIS COULD NOT LIVE SIDE BY SIDE. THIS POINT OF VIEW WAS FURTHER HEIGHTENED BY THE GENOCIDE. MANY OF THESE "EXPERTS" EVEN SUGGESTED THAT HUTUS AND TUTSIS SHOULD BE SEPARATED COMPLETELY, WITH SOME RECOMMENDING THAT ALL HUTUS SHOULD MOVE TO BURUNDI AND ALL TUTSIS TO RWANDA. OTHERS PROPOSED THAT BURUNDI SHOULD BE ANNEXED BY TANZANIA AND RWANDA BY UGANDA.

HUTU AND TUTSI CURRENTLY COEXIST. THIS IS A LESSON THAT ISRAEL COULD LEARN FROM.

THE RWANDAN POLITICAL SYSTEM, FOLLOWING THE GENOCIDE, REFUSED TO MAKE IDENTITY POLITICS A FACTOR. THE MAJORITY OF THOSE WHO WERE INVOLVED IN THE GENOCIDE WERE PARDONED, LEAVING ONLY THE LEADERS TO FACE CRIMINAL CHARGES.

THE RWANDAN PATRIOTIC FRONT HAS WORKED HARD TO MAKE SURE THAT RWANDANS NO LONGER IDENTIFY THEMSELVES BY THEIR HUTU OR TUTSI STATUS, BUT RATHER VIEW THEMSELVES AS A WHOLE NATION WITH A UNIFIED PAST, PRESENT, AND FUTURE.

IN ISRAEL, CITIZENSHIP IS LARGELY BASED ON RELIGION AND ETHNICITY, WHICH IS INTENDED TO MAINTAIN A JEWISH MAJORITY IN THE STATE. PALESTINIANS ARE DENIED ANY RIGHTS AND TREATED AS A CONQUERED AND SUBORDINATE POPULATION. THESE TERRITORIES ARE COMPARABLE TO THE BANTUSTANS OF APARTHEID SOUTH AFRICA AND NATIVE RESERVES OF THE UNITED STATES AND CANADA, AND ARE A SOURCE OF RECRUITMENT FOR HAMAS.

THE AMERICAN AND CANADIAN GOVERNMENTS WERE SUCCESSFUL IN SUBJUGATING AND TAKING CONTROL OF INDIGENOUS LAND THROUGH A POLICY OF GENOCIDE, LEAVING FEW SURVIVORS. IS ISRAEL CAPABLE OF SUCH A FEAT?

ISRAEL DOES NOT HAVE TO RESORT TO THE SAME TACTICS AS ADOLF HITLER, NORTH AMERICAN SETTLERS, OR APARTHEID SOUTH AFRICA TO BE SECURE. PERMITTING FULL AUTONOMY FOR PALESTINIANS IN GAZA AND THE WEST BANK (THE TWO-STATES SOLUTION) IS THE ONLY FAIR SOLUTION. HOWEVER, THIS NECESSITATES ISRAEL RE-ENVISIONING ITSELF NOT AS AN ETHNO-RELIGIOUS NATION BUT AS A LIBERAL DEMOCRATIC ONE.

IT MUST ABSTAIN FROM BUILDING A MODERN EUROPEAN STATE FOUNDED ON ETHNIC CLEANSING AND INSTEAD WORK TOWARDS CONSTRUCTING A NATION LIKE RWANDA AND SOUTH AFRICA HAVE DONE.

Unleashing the Power of Social Media: How it Shaped the Response on "Al-Aqsa Flood" Operation

In an era of uncertainty and division, verifying information and finding trustworthy sources has become increasingly challenging. Social media platforms have emerged as crucial information hubs, simultaneously serving as powerful tools and potential threats. These platforms have been exploited by major nations and governments to manipulate public opinion, using algorithms to sway narratives, distort facts, and propagate false and misleading content.

Consequently, social media has become a battleground, where political, economic, social, and cultural interests clash in a virtual war for control over collective consciousness.

THE RISE OF SOCIAL MEDIA..AKA "NETWORK WARFARE"

FOR OVER TWO DECADES, EXPERTS HAVE BEEN ANTICIPATING THE EMERGENCE OF "NETWORK WARFARE" IN THE 21ST CENTURY. THIS FORM OF WARFARE DOES NOT INVOLVE CYBER ATTACKS OR DIRECT ASSAULTS ON INFORMATION TECHNOLOGY OR COMMUNICATION SYSTEMS. INSTEAD, IT FOCUSES ON DELIBERATELY MANIPULATING THE PERCEPTIONS OF A SPECIFIC GROUP, CAUSING HARM TO THE TARGET OF THE ATTACK. IN OUR CURRENT DIGITAL AGE, THERE IS NO LONGER A NEED FOR PHYSICAL VIOLENCE TO ELIMINATE A COMPETITOR OR ACHIEVE VICTORY IN A GROUND WAR. THIS IS DUE TO THE EXISTENCE OF A GLOBAL DIGITAL SYSTEM THAT CONTROLS BILLIONS OF PEOPLE AND THE IMMENSE POWER OF "INFORMATION WARFARE," WHICH CAN BE UTILIZED BY COUNTRIES, COMPANIES, SMALL GROUPS, AND EVEN INDIVIDUALS.

Prior to 2011, there was a belief that social media served solely commercial purposes and its impact on major events in the Middle East and North Africa region that year came as a surprise. It became clear that disregarding social media was no longer an option. On the other hand, completely shutting down internet access proved to be an ineffective approach. People now have various means of creating, receiving, and sharing information. As a result, social media has become a valuable tool for detecting potential security threats and harmful activities, particularly when utilized by anti-government groups, opposition states, or terrorist organizations.

THE IMPORTANCE AND DANGER OF SOCIAL MEDIA

PEOPE TEND TO DOWNPLAY THE SIGNIFICANCE OF SOCIAL MEDIA PLATFORMS, THESE PLATFORMS ARE NOW USED FOR ACCESSING NEWS AND LATEST COVERAGE ON WORLD EVENTS. RECENT STUDIES INDICATE THAT APPROXIMATELY 30% OF INDIVIDUALS AGED 18 TO 24 CONSIDER SOCIAL MEDIA AS THEIR PRIMARY SOURCE OF NEWS.

THIS TREND HIGHLIGHTS THE INFLUENCE THESE PLATFORMS HAVE ON SHAPING OPINIONS, EMOTIONS, AND BEHAVIOR. IT IS WORTH NOTING THAT THESE PLATFORMS CAN BE USED TO MANIPULATE USERS THROUGH THE DISSEMINATION OF BOTH ACCURATE AND FALSE INFORMATION. BY STRATEGICALLY SHARING REPETITIVE NARRATIVES AND EMPLOYING TARGETED PAID ADVERTISEMENTS AND DIRECT COMMUNICATION, THESE PLATFORMS AIM TO ACHIEVE MAXIMUM IMPACT. FURTHERMORE, SOCIAL MEDIA ALGORITHMS ARE UTILIZED TO CONTROL THE ORGANIZATION AND RANKING OF CONTENT, ENSURING THAT ONLY INFORMATION ALIGNED WITH SPECIFIC GOALS

REACHES USERS WHILE PREVENTING CONTENT THAT DOES NOT SERVE THOSE GOALS FROM REACHING THEM.

MANY NATIONS COMMONLY UTILIZE SOCIAL MEDIA AS A STRATEGIC TOOL IN VARIOUS DOMAINS AND CRITICAL JUNCTURES TO SHAPE THEIR IMAGE DURING TIMES OF CRISES. WE OBSERVE THAT ACTORS WHO INFLUENCE PUBLIC PERCEPTION ARE COMMITTED TO DEPLOYING THIS TOOL IN DIVERSE DIRECTIONS, INCLUDING:

POLITICAL ORIENTATIONS: SOCIAL MEDIA IS EMPLOYED TO PROMOTE A SPECIFIC POLITICAL AGENDA AND EXERT INFLUENCE, SUCH AS MANIPULATING ELECTION OUTCOMES (AS INDICATED BY AMERICAN REPORTS ON RUSSIAN INTERFERENCE IN THE 2016 US ELECTIONS), DESTABILIZING POLITICAL SYSTEMS, OR ERODING PUBLIC TRUST IN THE GOVERNMENT. THESE ACTORS CONSIST OF POLITICAL ALLIANCES BETWEEN COUNTRIES, INDIVIDUAL NATIONS, POLITICAL PARTIES, OR EVEN MILITARY FACTIONS.

ECONOMIC ORIENTATIONS: THE UNDERLYING MOTIVE FOR THE SOCIAL MEDIA WARFARE IN THIS CONTEXT IS TYPICALLY FINANCIAL. THE INDUSTRIAL GROUPS OR SECTORS DRIVING THIS CONFLICT SEEK TO ASSERT THEIR INTERESTS, GAIN ADVANTAGES, INFLICT HARM ON OTHERS, AND TARNISH THEIR REPUTATIONS. IT IS USUALLY LARGER COMPANIES THAT BECOME THE VICTIMS OF THIS WARFARE.

UNIQUE INTERESTS DRIVING TRENDS: BESIDES POLITICAL AND ECONOMIC MOTIVATIONS, THERE EXIST OTHER REASONS FOR ENGAGING IN THE SOCIAL MEDIA BATTLE. THESE INCLUDE GROUPS WITH SPECIFIC OBJECTIVES THAT AIM TO EXERT INFLUENCE OVER PUBLIC OPINION. EXAMPLES OF SUCH GROUPS ARE TERRORIST ORGANIZATIONS OR POLITICAL ENTITIES SEEKING TO RECRUIT MORE FOLLOWERS TO ACCOMPLISH THEIR GOALS.

DIVERSE MOTIVATIONS GUIDING ACTIONS: THERE ARE GROUPS THAT ACTIVELY PARTICIPATE IN THIS BATTLE DUE TO THEIR SHARED INTERESTS IN MULTIPLE AREAS. IN 2020, IT WAS DISCOVERED THAT PRIVATE COMPANIES FROM 48 COUNTRIES OPERATE ON SOCIAL MEDIA PLATFORMS ON THEIR OWN BEHALF, WITH AN ANNUAL EXPENDITURE OF UP TO 60 MILLION US DOLLARS.

"AL-AQSA FLOOD" OPERATION...
NUMEROUS AMERICAN NEWSPAPERS, AS WELL AS PRESIDENT JOE BIDEN, PROPAGATED MISLEADING ISRAELI NARRATIVES REGARDING THE "AL-AQSA FLOOD" OPERATION AND THE SUBSEQUENT BOMBING OF GAZA. THESE NARRATIVES DISTORTED THE TRUE STORY OF THE WAR CRIMES, GENOCIDE, AND ISRAELI VIOLATIONS OF INTERNATIONAL CONVENTIONS AND LAWS OCCURRING IN GAZA.

THE PROLIFERATION OF MISINFORMATION, FALSE CONTENT, AND HATE SPEECH ON SOCIAL MEDIA PLATFORMS HAS REACHED UNPRECEDENTED LEVELS. THIS KIND OF CONTENT HAS NOT ONLY FUELED MORE VIOLENCE BUT HAS ALSO PROVIDED SUPPORT FOR WAR CRIMES AND INFLUENCED REAL-WORLD POLICY DECISIONS. SOCIAL MEDIA HAS BECOME A CATALYST FOR VIOLENCE.

IN THIS UNPARALLELED CONFLICT, WHERE PALESTINIAN VOICES AND STORIES ARE DISREGARDED, NARRATIVES AND REPORTING PRACTICES HAVE PERPETUATED THE DEHUMANIZATION OF THE PALESTINIAN PEOPLE AND UNDERMINED THEIR SUFFERING. DECISIONS ARE BEING MADE BASED ON INCOMPLETE INFORMATION AND EVENTS TAKEN OUT OF CONTEXT.

THE ISRAELI GOVERNMENT IS CURRENTLY ENGAGED IN A PRECISE COURSE OF ACTION. FOLLOWING THE ATTACK ON OCTOBER 7, ALL COMMUNICATION CHANNELS WITH PALESTINE HAVE BEEN SEVERED, AND A WIDESPREAD SOCIAL MEDIA CAMPAIGN HAS BEEN INITIATED IN WESTERN COUNTRIES SUCH AS FRANCE, GERMANY, THE UNITED STATES, AND THE UNITED KINGDOM. THE MAIN OBJECTIVE OF THIS CAMPAIGN IS TO GARNER SUPPORT FOR THE ISRAELI MILITARY'S RESPONSE AGAINST HAMAS. TO ACHIEVE THIS GOAL, THE GOVERNMENT HAS INVESTED SIGNIFICANT FUNDS, AMOUNTING TO TENS OF MILLIONS OF DOLLARS, IN NUMEROUS ADVERTISEMENTS FEATURING IMAGES OF THE VIOLENCE THAT ALLEGEDLY TOOK PLACE ON OCTOBER 7 WITHIN ISRAEL.

THESE ADS HAVE BEEN STRATEGICALLY PLACED ON PLATFORMS LIKE FACEBOOK AND YOUTUBE, WITH THE INTENT OF PORTRAYING HAMAS AS AN "EVIL TERRORIST GROUP." THE PROMOTION OF THESE ADVERTISEMENTS HAS RESULTED IN THEIR RAPID DISSEMINATION, LEADING TO THE ASSOCIATION OF THE NAMES "HAMAS" AND "ISIS." NATURALLY,

THE FREQUENCY OF THESE ANNOUNCEMENTS INTENSIFIED AFTER THE TARGETING OF AL-AHLI BAPTIST HOSPITAL IN THE GAZA STRIP. ISRAEL MADE EXTENSIVE EFFORTS TO ABSOLVE ITSELF OF ANY RESPONSIBILITY, INSTEAD ATTRIBUTING THE INCIDENT TO PALESTINIAN FACTIONS.

Unleashing the Power of Social Media: How it Shaped the Response on "Al-Aqsa Flood" Operation

Egypt has always played an important role in the Palestinian conflict. A conflict that is seen as the most crucial issue in the Middle East, and Palestine is also considered a direct concern for Egyptian national security. However, the ongoing conflict between Israel and Gaza has introduced new dimensions that have influenced Egypt's stance and actions. One such dimension is the concept of "sovereignty," which has now become a "red line" that cannot be crossed under any circumstances. The recent Israeli moves during this conflict have revealed their strategic plans to establish the "Greater Gaza" project, which would encroach upon Egyptian territory. We explore why Egypt views the current conflict in Gaza as a threat to its sovereignty

AND WHY IT EMPHASIZES THE CONCEPT OF THE "RED LINE."

"GREATER GAZA"...

ON TUESDAY, OCTOBER 24TH, CALCALIST MAGAZINE, WHICH IS AFFILIATED WITH THE ISRAELI NEWSPAPER YEDIOTH AHRONOTH, RELEASED A LEAKED REPORT THAT EXPOSED THE ISRAELI MINISTRY OF INTELLIGENCE'S PUSH FOR THE ISRAELI GOVERNMENT TO INITIATE THE IMPLEMENTATION OF A PLAN TO FORCIBLY RELOCATE PALESTINIANS TO EGYPTIAN TERRITORY. SPECIFICALLY, THE PLAN AIMS TO MOVE PALESTINIANS FROM RAFAH IN EGYPT TO THE CITY OF AL-ARISH, WHICH IS CONSIDERED A SECURE AND RESTRICTED AREA UNDER EGYPTIAN ADMINISTRATION. IN RETURN, ISRAEL WOULD MAINTAIN ITS OCCUPATION OF THE WELL-KNOWN GAZA STRIP AREA AND GRANT SOME PALESTINIANS THERE PERMANENT ISRAELI CITIZENSHIP.

THE PLAN FOR ESTABLISHING A STATE CALLED "GREATER GAZA" IS DIVIDED INTO THREE PHASES: (1) SETTING UP TEMPORARY SETTLEMENTS IN THE SOUTHWEST OF THE GAZA STRIP, SPECIFICALLY IN SINAI.

(2) Creating a humanitarian corridor to provide assistance to the population.

(3) Constructing cities in North Sinai.

These stages aim to transition Gaza's reliance to the Egyptian administration, with the responsibility of developing the new region falling on the Egyptian economy. This includes rebuilding infrastructure, power lines, and providing livelihoods for the Palestinians who have been displaced.

A leaked document from the Ministry of Foreign Affairs outlines the initial steps taken by Israeli research centers that align with the extreme right-wing movement, such as the Israeli "Misgav" Center. The document, titled "Economic Aspects of the Final Settlement and Rehabilitation Plan in Egypt," focuses on the residents of the Gaza Strip and their economic prospects.

According to the research, Egypt has the potential, both in terms of infrastructure and demographics, to accommodate the entire population of the Gaza Strip,

WHICH CONSISTS OF APPROXIMATELY TWO MILLION PALESTINIANS. THIS COULD BE ACHIEVED BY PROVIDING EGYPT WITH THE NECESSARY FINANCIAL ASSISTANCE TO REHABILITATE THE RESIDENTS OF GAZA IN THE SINAI REGION. THE STUDY ALSO HIGHLIGHTED THAT THERE ARE SIX MILLION UNOCCUPIED HOUSING UNITS IN SINAI, WHICH COULD EASILY ACCOMMODATE THE GAZA RESIDENTS. NOTING THAT THE POPULATION OF GAZA REPRESENTS LESS THAN 2% OF EGYPT'S TOTAL POPULATION.

"EGYPT'S REJECTION"

THE EGYPTIAN GOVERNMENT IS AWARE THAT THE MILITARY OPERATION IS PART OF AN ISRAELI STRATEGY THAT MAY NOT BE OFFICIALLY ANNOUNCED YET, BUT IS EVIDENT IN CERTAIN ISRAELI RESEARCH MATERIALS AND THE ISRAELI MINISTRY OF INTELLIGENCE. THIS STRATEGY, AS PREVIOUSLY MENTIONED, CENTERS AROUND THE IDEA OF "RELOCATING THE POPULATION OF THE GAZA STRIP TO SINAI." IT SHOULD BE NOTED THAT EGYPT HAS OFFICIALLY REJECTED THIS PLAN, EMPHASIZING ITS OPPOSITION TO

FORCED DISPLACEMENT. THIS STANCE HAS BEEN SUPPORTED BY VARIOUS POLITICAL GROUPS THROUGH PROTESTS CONDEMNING THE PROPOSED PLANS. THE EGYPTIAN LEADERSHIP VIEWS ANY ENCROACHMENT ON EGYPTIAN SOVEREIGNTY AS A "RED LINE" THAT CANNOT BE COMPROMISED.

THE PHILADELPHIA CORRIDOR..

AN EXAMPLE OF THE SERIOUSNESS OF THE EGYPTIANS TOWARDS THEIR SOVEREIGNTY CAN BE VIEWED WHEN EGYPTIAN AUTHORITIES CAUTIONED ISRAELIS AGAINST ANY ACTIVITIES OCCURRING IN THE PHILADELPHIA CORRIDOR DURING THE GROUND OFFENSIVE INTO THE GAZA STRIP. THIS AREA IS PROTECTED BY THE EGYPT-ISRAEL PEACE TREATY OF 1979.

CAIRO ISSUED THE WARNING AHEAD OF ANY ISRAELI PLANS OF INVASION OF THE GAZA STRIP, DUE TO THE PHILADELPHIA CORRIDOR BEING AN INTEGRAL PART OF THE PEACE TREATY.

ACCORDING TO A SOURCE, EGYPT WOULD NOT TOLERATE ANY ISRAELI INVASION OF THE PASSAGEWAY, FOR IT WOULD BE A BREACH OF INTERNATIONAL AGREEMENT.

ADDITIONALLY, THE SOURCE REPORTED THAT CAIRO HAD EXPRESSED DOUBT TO ISRAEL REGARDING THE RECENT ATTACK ON AN EGYPTIAN MILITARY SURVEILLANCE TOWER CLOSE TO THE GAZA STRIP, WHICH ISRAEL MENTIONED IT HAD FIRED UPON "INADVERTENTLY".

THE SOURCE REPORTED THAT THE EGYPTIAN PROBES SUGGEST THAT THE ISRAELI ATTACK WAS INTENTIONAL. IT WAS ALLEGEDLY INTENDED TO INDUCE EGYPT TO MAKE A UNILATERAL DECISION TO SHUT DOWN THE RAFAH FRONTIER CROSSING, WHICH WOULD EVOKE PALESTINIAN AND ARAB IRE.

ITS WORTH NOTING THAT EGYPT HAS DEMANDED AN END TO THE ISRAELI MILITARY'S BOMBARDMENT OF CIVILIANS IN GAZA SINCE THE OUTBREAK OF THE WAR THREE WEEKS AGO, AND THE EGYPTIAN GOVERNMENT HAS ALSO WARNED THAT A GROUND INVASION OF THE GAZA STRIP WOULD BRING ABOUT NEVER-BEFORE-SEEN HUMANITARIAN CRISIS.

UNVEILING THE HIDDEN ORIGINS: THE DARK TRUTH ABOUT ZIONISM AND ITS DISTINCTION FROM JUDAISM

What sets apart Jews from Zionists...and what distinguishes them fundamentally? Many beliefs center around connecting Jews with Zionists or vice versa, but this is an inaccurate notion based solely on uninformed opinions. In this blog, we will discover the historical origins of Jews and the Zionists.

Judaism is an ancient celestial religion, and its holy scripture is the Torah, which was revealed to Moses - may peace be upon him -. In Surat Al-A'raf, God - The Almighty - said, "He said, 'O Moses, I have chosen you above the people with My revelations and My words. So take what I have given you and be among the grateful.'" Jewish people are who follow a sacred text and have their own beliefs and religion.

ZIONISM IS AN INTERNATIONAL MOVEMENT WHOSE INITIAL GOAL WAS TO RELOCATE ALL JEWS WORLDWIDE TO THE STATE OF PALESTINE, WHICH INCLUDES MOUNT ZION IN THE SOUTHERN PART OF JERUSALEM. THEY CLAIM THAT THIS LAND IS THE PROMISED LAND. THE TERM "ZION" IS MENTIONED IN THE BOOK OF ISAIAH, THE TWELFTH BOOK OF THE TORAH.

JUDAISM..

IN 1451 BC, A GROUP OF INDIVIDUALS REFERRED TO AS THE SONS OF JUDAH INHABITED THE REGION OF CANAAN. CANAAN WAS A LAND SITUATED BETWEEN THE EASTERN COAST OF THE MEDITERRANEAN SEA AND THE JORDAN RIVER. THESE INDIVIDUALS WERE KNOWN AS THE HEBREWS AND RESIDED IN THE HEBRON AREA OF PALESTINE FROM 1991 TO 1706 BC.

THE DESCENDANTS OF JACOB, MAY PEACE BE UPON HIM, ARE KNOWN AS THE CHILDREN OF ISRAEL AND ARE COMPRISED OF TWELVE TRIBES: REUBEN, SIMEON, LEVI, JUDAH, ISACHAR, ZEBULUN, DAN, GAD, NAPHTALI, ASHER, JOSEPH, AND BENJAMIN.

AFTER THEIR JOURNEY TO EGYPT AND DEPARTURE FROM THE LAND OF CANAAN, GOD, REFERRED TO AS JEHOVAH IN THE OLD TESTAMENT, THE BIBLE, THE TORAH, AND MENTIONED IN THE BOOK OF EXODUS THROUGH MOSES, WAS SENT TO GUIDE THEM. EVENTUALLY, THEY RETURNED TO THE LAND OF CANAAN AFTER ENDURING 400 YEARS. FOLLOWING THEIR FORTY-YEAR SENTENCE TO WANDER THE LAND, CANAAN WAS ONCE AGAIN CONQUERED UNDER PROPHET JOSHUA BIN NUN. THE TWELVE TRIBES THEN DISPERSED THROUGHOUT THE LAND. IN 1000 BC, KING TALUT RULED OVER CANAAN, FOLLOWED BY THE ARRIVAL OF PROPHET DAVID AND LATER PROPHET SOLOMON.

SUBSEQUENTLY, THE CHILDREN OF ISRAEL CAME UNDER THE RULE OF KING SHALMANESER V IN THE FIFTH CENTURY BC. UNFORTUNATELY, THERE ARE NO HISTORICAL RECORDS DOCUMENTING THE WHEREABOUTS OR DISAPPEARANCE OF THESE TRIBES THEREAFTER.

ZIONISM..

ZIONISM EMERGED IN THE LATE 19TH CENTURY AD AS A POLITICAL MOVEMENT INITIATED BY EUROPEAN JEWS. IT AIMED TO ENCOURAGE JEWISH PEOPLE WORLDWIDE TO RELOCATE TO PALESTINE. THE VISIONARY LEADER OF THIS MOVEMENT WAS HERZL, A JEWISH ADVOCATE WHO PLAYED A SIGNIFICANT ROLE IN ESTABLISHING THE ZIONIST STATE IN 1948. THE INAUGURAL CONFERENCE TOOK PLACE IN BASEL, SWITZERLAND, IN 1897, LAYING THE FOUNDATION FOR INCREASED JEWISH MIGRATION TO PALESTINE WITH THE BACKING OF THE UNITED STATES AND SUPPORT FOR ZIONIST ECONOMIC INITIATIVES.

THREE MEETINGS TOOK PLACE IN BASEL, WITH ONE GATHERING HELD IN LONDON UNDER HERZL'S GUIDANCE. HERZL URGED THE PUBLIC TO CONTRIBUTE AND BACK THE ECONOMIC DEVELOPMENT OF THE FORTHCOMING STATE. HE ALSO SHARED THE OUTCOMES OF HIS DISCUSSIONS WITH GERMANY'S KAISER. THESE EVENTS OCCURRED DURING THE TIME OF THE OTTOMAN EMPIRE, UNDER SULTAN ABDUL HAMID II'S RULE.

THE STORY OF THEODOR HERZ... THE GODFATHER OF ZIONISM...

IN 1894, THE FRENCH LEGAL SYSTEM ACCUSED ALFRED DREYFUS, A JEWISH OFFICER, OF COMMITTING ACTS OF TREASON. DURING THE TRIAL PROCEEDINGS, HERZL PERSONALLY HEARD THE CROWD CHANTING PHRASES LIKE "DEATH TO THE JEWS." THIS EXPERIENCE SOLIDIFIED HIS BELIEF THAT IT WAS IMPOSSIBLE FOR JEWS TO ASSIMILATE INTO CHRISTIAN SOCIETIES AND THAT THE ONLY SOLUTION TO THE "JEWISH PROBLEM" WAS THE ESTABLISHMENT OF A NATIONAL HOMELAND FOR JEWS. INFLUENCED BY DREYFUS'S CASE, HERZL WROTE A BOOK TITLED "THE JEWISH STATE" IN 1896.

IN THIS BOOK, HE AIMED TO DEMONSTRATE THAT JEWS WERE A DISTINCT NATION AND THAT THEIR STRUGGLES SHOULD BE VIEWED AS A NATIONAL ISSUE, SIMILAR TO THE STRUGGLES FACED BY OTHER OPPRESSED ETHNIC GROUPS.

IN 1897, HE ESTABLISHED A NEWSPAPER AS A PLATFORM FOR THE ZIONIST MOVEMENT. A SIGNIFICANT EVENT TOOK PLACE IN AUGUST OF THAT YEAR WHEN THE FIRST ZIONIST CONFERENCE CONVENED IN BASEL, SWITZERLAND. OVER TWO HUNDRED INDIVIDUALS FROM AROUND THE GLOBE ATTENDED THIS CONFERENCE. IT WAS DURING THIS GATHERING THAT THE INITIAL CHARTER OF THE ZIONIST MOVEMENT WAS DRAFTED, AND A CRUCIAL DECISION WAS MADE TO PURSUE THE ESTABLISHMENT OF A NATIONAL HOMELAND FOR JEWS IN PALESTINE. ADDITIONALLY, THE CONFERENCE GAVE ITS APPROVAL TO THE ZIONIST FLAG AND NATIONAL ANTHEM.

IN 1898, HERZL MADE AN ATTEMPT TO PERSUADE

THE GERMAN EMPEROR TO INTERVENE WITH THE OTTOMAN SULTAN ABDUL HAMID, URGING HIM TO SUPPORT THE CREATION OF A JEWISH COMPANY IN PALESTINE UNDER GERMAN PROTECTION. HOWEVER, THE EMPEROR'S RESPONSE WAS LUKEWARM, AND HE MADE NO PROMISES DURING THEIR MEETING. IT BECAME EVIDENT TO HERZL THAT GERMANY LACKED THE CAPACITY TO ADDRESS THIS MATTER.

IN 1901, WITH GERMANY'S STANCE IN MIND, HERZL ATTEMPTED TO ARRANGE A MEETING WITH SULTAN ABDUL HAMID. HIS GOAL WAS TO CONVINCE THE SULTAN TO ALLOW JEWISH IMMIGRATION TO PALESTINE AND GRANT THEM SELF-GOVERNANCE. AS AN INCENTIVE, HERZL HINTED AT FINANCIAL ASSISTANCE THAT COULD POTENTIALLY RESCUE THE OTTOMAN EMPIRE FROM ITS FINANCIAL TROUBLES. HOWEVER, THE SULTAN REJECTED HERZL'S PROPOSAL.

EVEN WITH THE SULTAN'S REFUSAL, JEWISH MIGRATION TO PALESTINE COMMENCED WITH TWO CONSECUTIVE WAVES. THE INITIAL WAVE SPANNED FROM 1882 TO 1904, WITH AROUND 25,000 IMMIGRANTS, PREDOMINANTLY RUSSIAN JEWS, RELOCATING TO PALESTINE. THE SUBSEQUENT WAVE, OCCURRING FROM 1904 TO 1913, SAW APPROXIMATELY 30,000 RUSSIAN JEWS DISPLACED TO PALESTINE. MEANWHILE, HERZL ENGAGED IN COMMUNICATION WITH JOSEPH CHAMBERLAIN, THE SECRETARY OF THE BRITISH EMPIRE, AND PRESENTED TO HIM THE CONCEPT OF RELOCATING JEWS TO EITHER CYPRUS OR THE SINAI PENINSULA. THE BRITISH AUTHORITIES AGREED TO THE FUNDAMENTAL PRINCIPLE OF THIS COLONIAL PROJECT PROPOSED BY THE ZIONISTS.

ULTIMATELY, THE DECISION WAS MADE TO FOCUS ON THE SINAI PENINSULA. IN 1903, LORD CROMER, THE BRITISH COMMISSIONER TO EGYPT, ESTABLISHED A COMMITTEE TO ASSESS THE FEASIBILITY OF SETTLING JEWS IN SINAI.

THE COMMITTEE DETERMINED THAT IT WAS SUITABLE FOR THE JEWISH PROJECT AND WOULD SERVE AS THE INITIAL STEP IN ESTABLISHING JEWISH COMMUNITIES IN AL-ARISH. HOWEVER, LORD CROMER DID NOT SUPPORT THIS ENDEAVOR, AND BOTH EGYPT AND THE OTTOMAN EMPIRE OPPOSED THE PROJECT.

SUBSEQUENTLY, BRITAIN EXTENDED AN OFFER TO THE JEWISH COMMUNITY TO CARRY OUT THEIR SETTLEMENT PROJECT IN UGANDA, LOCATED IN EAST AFRICA. THE ZIONISTS HAD DIFFERING OPINIONS ON THIS MATTER. SOME PERCEIVED IT AS A TRIUMPH, BELIEVING THAT THE IDEA OF GATHERING JEWS IN A NATIONAL HOMELAND HAD BEEN ACCOMPLISHED. CONVERSELY, OTHERS REGARDED IT AS A BETRAYAL OF THE ZIONIST IDEOLOGY, AS THEY FIRMLY BELIEVED THAT PALESTINE WAS THE TRUE PROMISED LAND.

IN 1903, THEODOR HERZL, THE VISIONARY AND CREATOR OF ZIONISM, PASSED AWAY. FOLLOWING HIS DEATH, IN 1905, THE SEVENTH ZIONIST CONGRESS UNANIMOUSLY MADE THE DECISION TO OPPOSE ANY ATTEMPTS TO ESTABLISH SETTLEMENTS OUTSIDE OF PALESTINE. THIS DECISION SET IN MOTION A SERIES OF EVENTS THAT ULTIMATELY LED TO THE DECLARATION OF THE ZIONIST STATE ON MAY 14, 1948.

FINALLY, AFTER EXAMING THE HISTORY OF BOTH, IT IS EVIDENT THAT ZIONISM IS NOT A RELIGION BUT AN INTERNATIONAL MOVEMENT COMMENCED BY SOME JEWISH INDIVIDUALS FROM THE PRIOR CENTURY, IT IS IMPORTANT TO MAKE THE DISTINGUISH BETWEEN BOTH. IF YOU OPPOSE ZIONISM, HOW COULD YOU BE CONSIDERED AN ANTI-SEMITE? YOU ARE MERELY OPPOSING AN IDEAOLOGY, A SCHOOL OF THOUGHT.

War in Gaza: Israeli Power Display Between Arrogance and Vengence

THE ONGOING CONFLICT IN GAZA PERSISTS NOT SOLELY BECAUSE OF A DESIRED GOAL OR PURPOSE, BUT ITS AIM IS ONLY TO ENACT VENGENCE ON THE PALESTINIAN PEOPLE - AN ATTITUDE OF ARROGANCE AND HUBRIS. THIS MINDSET, WHICH IS EVEN MORE DETRIMENTAL THAN ANY EXTERNAL THREAT, DOMINATES ISRAEL'S POLICY AND INFLUENCES ITS POLITICAL AND MILITARY LEADERS. DESPITE THE SIGNIFICANT HARM IT HAS CAUSED ISRAEL OVER THE YEARS, INCLUDING THE LOSS OF COUNTLESS ISRAELI LIVES, THESE LEADERS STUBBORNLY CLING TO THIS DESTRUCTIVE VIOLENCE.

DURING THE PERIOD PRECEDING THE OCTOBER 1973 CONFLICT, FORMER EGYPTIAN PRESIDENT ANWAR SADAT PUT FORTH MULTIPLE PEACE PROPOSALS, ALL OF WHICH WERE DISDAINFULLY DISMISSED BY THE GOVERNMENT LED BY GOLDA MEIR. CONSEQUENTLY, THE 6TH OF OCTOBER WAR ENSUED, RESULTING IN THE LOSS OF 2,689 ISRAELI LIVES AND LEAVING 7,251 INDIVIDUALS WOUNDED.

IN 2002, THE ARABS OFFERED ISRAEL A COMPLETE AND COMPREHENSIVE PEACE INITIATIVE WITH THE ENTIRE ARAB NATION, AND WITHIN A SHORT PERIOD IT TURNED INTO AN INITIATIVE ON BEHALF OF 57 ISLAMIC COUNTRIES, BUT IT REJECTED IT IN PRACTICE AND PREFERRED TO MANAGE THE CONFLICT.

TWO MONTHS AGO, PRIME MINISTER BENJAMIN NETANYAHU RECEIVED A WARNING ABOUT THE CONSEQUENCES OF HIS CURRENT POLICIES. THESE POLICIES HAVE LED TO UNREST AMONG SETTLERS IN THE WEST BANK AND JERUSALEM, VIOLATED THE SANCTITY OF AL-AQSA MOSQUE, ABUSED PALESTINIAN PRISONERS IN PRISONS. IT WAS PREDICTED THAT THESE ACTIONS WOULD RESULT IN A DANGEROUS ESCALATION OF SECURITY, AND UNFORTUNATELY, THAT PREDICTION CAME TRUE. AN EXPLOSION OCCURRED, RESULTING IN THE DEATH OF 1,400 ISRAELIS IN JUST ONE DAY. WHILE IT IS ACKNOWLEDGED THAT SOME PALESTINIANS WERE RESPONSIBLE FOR THESE DEATHS, THE ISRAELI RESPONSE WAS DISPROPORTIONATELY BRUTAL AND DEVASTATING.

Amos Harel, a renowned Israeli writer and military affairs editor of the newspaper "Haaretz," shared an interesting insight. He mentioned that in one of the session rooms at IDF chiefs of staff, there was a quote written on the wall by Karl von Clausewitz, a Prussian strategist considered one of the fathers of modern warfare. The quote stated that no one, especially not someone with strategic thinking, would initiate a war without clearly defining their objectives and how they plan to achieve them.

He further stated, "There is room for discussion on whether this statement is a prophetic critique regarding the reckless gamble made by Yahya Sinwar, the leader of Hamas in the Gaza Strip. However, these statements also warrant contemplation from the Israeli perspective, rather than simply dismissing them outright."

MANY INDIVIDUALS, EVEN THOSE WHO SUPPORT ISRAEL IN THE WESTERN WORLD, OBSERVE THE IMAGES OF CHARRED BODIES OF CHILDREN IN GAZA AND WITNESS THE SEVERE DISPLACEMENT OF HUNDREDS OF THOUSANDS OF GAZANS. THEY ALSO HEAR THE CRIES OF WOMEN AND THE AGONIZING MOANS OF MEN WHO HAVE LOST THEIR ENTIRE FAMILIES. IN LIGHT OF THESE CIRCUMSTANCES, THEY QUESTION WHY ISRAEL WOULD ENGAGE IN THIS SENSELESS ATTACK ON CIVILIANS, HOSPITALS, AND THE PATIENTS WITHIN THEM. UNFORTUNATELY, THEY STRUGGLE TO FIND AN ANSWER TO THIS PRESSING QUESTION.

FRIENDS OF ISRAEL AVOID CONFRONTATION WITH ITS LEADERS IN ORDER TO PREVENT THEM FROM BECOMING MORE AGGRESSIVE. INSTEAD, THEY CHOOSE TO OFFER ADVICE, RAISE AWARENESS, AND APPLY GENTLE, COMPASSIONATE PRESSURE. HOWEVER, THESE EFFORTS SEEM FUTILE.

WE ARE CURRENTLY WITNESSING A BRUTAL FORM OF RETRIBUTION, REMINISCENT OF THE BIBLICAL REFERENCE TO "AMALEK," STATED BY NETANYAHU IN ONE OF HIS SPEECHES AT THE ONSET OF THE WAR. THE QUOTE EMPHASIZES THE NEED TO OBLITERATE, AND SPARE NO ONE, NOT EVEN MEN, WOMEN, CHILDREN, INFANTS, ANIMALS, OR LIVESTOCK (1 SAMUEL 15:3).

THE ISSUE LIES IN THE FACT THAT ISRAELI LEADERS ADHERE TO THIS APPROACH WITHOUT CONSIDERING THE CONSEQUENCES IT MAY HAVE ON THE PALESTINIAN VICTIMS OR THE GLOBAL COMMUNITY. THIS PATTERN HAS BEEN EVIDENT THROUGHOUT ALL THE WARS, STARTING FROM THE 1948 NAKBA TO THE RECENT GAZA NAKBA. IT INADVERTENTLY CULTIVATES A NEW GENERATION FILLED WITH RESENTMENT AND ANIMOSITY, SURPASSING EVEN THAT OF HAMAS. CONSEQUENTLY, THESE INDIVIDUALS WILL UNDOUBTEDLY DEVISE THEIR OWN PLANS FOR REVENGE.

ISRAEL'S PROPAGANDA MACHINE: HOW LIES LED TO DEFEAT

INLIGHT OF THE ISRAELI AGGRESSION IN GAZA AND THE MEDIA COVERAGE OF THE EVENTS, THE DOCUMENTATION OF CONFLICTS HAS BECOME A TOP PRIORITY. WITH THE PROLIFERATION OF MEDIA TOOLS, INCLUDING VARIOUS SOCIAL MEDIA PLATFORMS ACCESSIBLE TO EVERYONE, THERE HAS BEEN A CLEAR DOMINANCE OF THE ISRAELI NARRATIVE. THIS NARRATIVE PORTRAYS ISRAEL AS A VICTIM, JUSTIFYING ITS AGGRESSION AND THE KILLING OF CIVILIANS. THIS DOMINANCE IS PARTICULARLY EVIDENT IN WESTERN MEDIA OUTLETS, WHICH HAVE GRADUALLY DECLINED IN CREDIBILITY. HOWEVER, THE PALESTINIAN AND ARAB NARRATIVES HAVE EXPOSED THE TRUTH BEHIND THESE NARRATIVES, LEADING TO ADVERSE RESULTS FOR ISRAEL. THIS SITUATION RAISES SEVERAL QUESTIONS ABOUT HOW ISRAEL SHAPES ITS MEDIA NARRATIVES, THE REASONS FOR ITS SIGNIFICANT INFLUENCE ON A GLOBAL SCALE, AND THE DECLINE IN WESTERN SUPPORT FOLLOWING A CAMPAIGN THAT BLINDLY ADOPTED THESE NARRATIVES, DAMAGING THE CREDIBILIT OF INTERNATIONAL NEWSPAPERS.

THE ISRAELI PROPAGANDA MACHINE

THE CONFLICT IN PALESTINE CENTERS AROUND THREE PRIMARY OBJECTIVES:

ACQUIRING TERRITORY

ERADICATING THE POPULATION

REWRITING HISTORY

ISRAEL HAS MADE SIGNIFICANT PROGRESS IN ACHIEVING THE FIRST TWO GOALS THROUGH THE PROCESS OF ETHNIC CLEANSING AND ONGOING SETTLEMENT EXPANSION. HOWEVER, IN PURSUIT OF THE THIRD OBJECTIVE, ISRAEL HAS BEEN ACTIVELY WORKING SINCE THE 1920S TO MANIPULATE THE NARRATIVE OF "VICTIMHOOD" IN ORDER TO RALLY PUBLIC SUPPORT FOR ITS AGGRESSIVE ACTIONS AGAINST THE PALESTINIANS AND THE VIOLATION OF THEIR RIGHTS. THIS DELIBERATE STRATEGY IS EMPLOYED TO ESTABLISH THE ISRAELI PERSPECTIVE AS THE ONLY TRUTH, PERPETUATING AN ENDLESS CYCLE OF VIOLENCE.

LOOKING BACK TO THE PERIOD BEFORE THE ESTABLISHMENT OF THE STATE OF ISRAEL, WE CAN TRACE THE ORIGINS OF THIS NARRATIVE OF PERSECUTION, WHICH ISRAEL FREQUENTLY INVOKES AND EQUATES WITH "ANTI-SEMITISM," TO THE LATE 19TH CENTURY. THEODOR HERZL, THE FOUNDER OF THE ZIONIST MOVEMENT, DREW UPON THE LONG HISTORY OF JEWISH PERSECUTION IN EUROPE TO LEGITIMIZE THE NATIONAL PROJECT OF CREATING THE STATE OF ISRAEL AND THE COLONIAL PRACTICES PURSUED BY ITS SETTLERS.

AFTER WORLD WAR II, THE ESTABLISHMENT OF THE STATE OF ISRAEL WAS JUSTIFIED BY USING PERSECUTION AS A PRETEXT. LOOKING AT THE DOCUMENT TITLED "DECLARATION OF THE ESTABLISHMENT OF THE STATE OF ISRAEL," IT STATES THAT THE HOLOCAUST, WHERE MILLIONS OF EUROPEAN JEWS WERE KILLED, HAS REINFORCED THE NEED FOR A JEWISH STATE IN ISRAEL TO PROVIDE A HOMELAND AND INDEPENDENCE FOR THE JEWISH PEOPLE. THIS WAS SEEN AS A SOLUTION TO THE PROBLEM OF JEWISH PEOPLE BEING WITHOUT A HOMELAND. IT WAS ALSO MENTIONED THAT THIS WOULD OPEN THE DOORS TO THEIR HOMELAND,

ALLOWING EVERY JEW TO HAVE A PLACE TO BELONG. AS A RESULT, VARIOUS COMPLEXES WERE DEVELOPED BY THE ISRAELIS, WHICH SERVED AS BOTH AN EXCUSE AND A MEANS OF PRESSURING THE GUILT-RIDDEN WEST FOR PAST PERSECUTION OF JEWS. THESE COMPLEXES INCLUDE THE "MASADA COMPLEX," REFERRING TO THE MASS SUICIDE COMMITTED BY JEWS DURING THE ROMAN ERA, THE "MASSACRE COMPLEX," THE "HITLER COMPLEX," AND THE "HOLOCAUST COMPLEX." THESE NAMES AND NARRATIVES ARE EMPLOYED TO PORTRAY VICTIMHOOD IN ORDER TO JUSTIFY ACTS OF AGGRESSION.

WITH THE PROLIFERATION OF SOCIAL MEDIA AND DIGITAL NEWS OUTLETS PREDOMINANTLY OWNED BY INDIVIDUALS OF JEWISH DESCENT, AND WITH THE ENDORSEMENT OF WESTERN GOVERNMENTS FOR ISRAEL, ALONG WITH SUBSTANTIAL INVESTMENTS AIMED AT IMPROVING ISRAEL'S REPUTATION, THE OCCUPATION STRATEGICALLY EMPLOYS THESE FACTORS TO DISSEMINATE ITS OWN PERSPECTIVE.

THIS IS ACHIEVED THROUGH THE UTILIZATION OF ALGORITHMS DESIGNED TO SHAPE THE NARRATIVE, INCLUDING THE DELIBERATE SELECTION OF SPECIFIC TERMINOLOGY AND PHRASES. FOR INSTANCE, DIFFERENTIATING BETWEEN THE VERBS "DEATH" AND "KILLING," WHERE "KILLING" DENOTES AN ACT OF AGGRESSION AGAINST ISRAEL, WHILE "DEATH" IS ATTRIBUTED TO PALESTINIANS AS A RESULT OF NON-VIOLENT CIRCUMSTANCES. SIMILARLY, THE TERM "TERRORIST" IS SELECTIVELY APPLIED TO HAMAS WHEN IT TARGETS CIVILIANS, YET IT IS NEVER UTILIZED IN REFERENCE TO ISRAEL'S DELIBERATE TARGETING OF CIVILIANS IN GAZA. ADDITIONALLY, ISRAELI DETAINEES RELEASED BY RESISTANCE FACTIONS ARE REFERRED TO AS "CHILDREN," WHEREAS PALESTINIANS RELEASED FROM OCCUPATION PRISONS ARE DESCRIBED AS "INDIVIDUALS UNDER 18 YEARS OF AGE."

THE PALESTINIAN "ENEMY" IS VIEWED AS LESS HUMANE IN THE ISRAELI NARRATIVE, LEADING TO THE MOBILIZATION OF SUPPORTERS AND SOLIDARITY. THIS, IN TURN, CAUSES THE INTERNATIONAL COMMUNITY TO TURN A BLIND EYE TO THE ENFORCEMENT OF INTERNATIONAL LAW AND THE PROTECTION OF BASIC HUMAN RIGHTS. AS A RESULT, DISCUSSING THE PALESTINIAN NARRATIVE BECOMES FUTILE, AS THERE IS A UNANIMOUS BELIEF THAT THEY DESERVE VIOLENCE RATHER THAN SYMPATHY.

CONSEQUENTLY, THIS MANIPULATION OF LANGUAGE NOT ONLY INFLUENCES THE PERCEPTION OF NEWS RECIPIENTS BUT ALSO OBSCURES THE PALESTINIAN NARRATIVE, IMPEDING ITS DISSEMINATION WITHIN THE DIGITAL REALM.

HAS ISRAEL LOST THE BATTLE OF PROPAGANDA?

THE DISCUSSION WITHIN ISRAEL IS INTENSIFYING REGARDING THE DIMINISHING REPUTATION OF THE COUNTRY AND ITS ONGOING CONFLICT WITH THE GAZA STRIP IN TERMS OF GLOBAL PUBLIC OPINION. INITIALLY, ISRAEL GARNERED SYMPATHY AND SUPPORT, BUT AS TIME WENT ON, THERE HAS BEEN A SHIFT IN PUBLIC SENTIMENT.

PEOPLE HAVE BEGUN OPPOSING AND CONDEMNING ISRAEL'S VIOLENT MILITARY ACTIONS IN GAZA, ALIGNING MORE WITH THE PALESTINIAN PERSPECTIVE. FURTHERMORE, EVEN WITHIN THE ARMY, DOUBTS ABOUT ITS EFFECTIVENESS HAVE ARISEN. ISRAEL RECOGNIZES THE IMPORTANCE OF MAINTAINING INTERNATIONAL SUPPORT TO SUSTAIN ITS PROLONGED WAR AGAINST THE GAZA STRIP, ESPECIALLY CONSIDERING THE DECLINING MORALE OF NETANYAHU AND HIS GOVERNMENT.

COMPLICATING MATTERS FURTHER IS THE ENDORSEMENT OF THE SITUATION IN GAZA BY THE UN AND OTHER INTERNATIONAL ORGANIZATIONS, WHICH HOLDS SIGNIFICANT CREDIBILITY WORLDWIDE. NATURALLY, ISRAEL IS DISSATISFIED WITH THESE INSTITUTIONS' POSITIONS, WHETHER IT BE THEIR BROADCASTING OF SCENES DEPICTING KILLINGS AND DESTRUCTION OR THEIR CALLS FOR A CEASEFIRE WHILE EXPRESSING DISMAY OVER THE HINDRANCE OF MEDICAL SUPPLIES, FOOD, FUEL, AND ELECTRICITY FROM ENTERING THE REGION.

Unveiling the Arrogance Shattering Israel's Foundation

The crisis Israel currently facing can be attributed largely to its arrogance and haughtiness. This exact traits play a significant role in the country's existential challenges.

Israeli journalist Gideon Levy, in an article for Haaretz newspaper, stated that Israel's sense of superiority is the underlying cause of all the events that have unfolded. He further added that Israelis believed they could act without consequences or retribution. Levy continued to express, "We persist without hesitation. We apprehend, eliminate, mistreat, plunder, shield settlers involved in massacres, visit Joseph's Tomb, Othniel's Tomb, and Joshua's Altar — all within Palestinian territories. And of course, we visit the 'Temple Mount' [Al-Aqsa Mosque], with over 5,000 Jews visiting during Sukkot. We harm innocent individuals, blind them, shatter their faces,

FORCIBLY REMOVE THEM, CONFISCATE THEIR LANDS, ABDUCT THEM FROM THEIR BEDS, AND ENGAGE IN ETHNIC CLEANSING. ADDITIONALLY, WE MAINTAIN AN UNJUSTIFIABLE BLOCKADE. AND EVERYTHING WILL PROCEED AS PLANNED."

HE ADDED THAT ISRAEL'S STRATEGY TO EXERT CONTROL OVER GAZA WAS BY OFFERING MINIMAL BENEFITS, SUCH AS A LIMITED NUMBER OF WORK PERMITS IN ISRAEL. HOWEVER, THIS TACTIC IS INSIGNIFICANT IN THE GRAND SCHEME OF THINGS AND IS CONTINGENT UPON COMPLIANCE. THE MAJORITY OF THE GAZA STRIP'S 2.3 MILLION PALESTINIANS LIVED IN IMPOVERISHED CONDITIONS. ACCORDING TO DATA FROM THE UNITED NATIONS IN 2021, WITH 71 PERCENT OF GAZANS RESIDE BELOW THE NATIONAL POVERTY LINE. ADDITIONALLY, 64 PERCENT EXPERIENCE FOOD INSECURITY.

THE FAILED ISRAELI STRATEGY..

SINCE 2006, ISRAEL HAS IMPLEMENTED A TWO-PRONGED APPROACH TOWARDS THE PALESTINIANS, WHICH HAS GARNERED SUPPORT FROM THE UNITED STATES AND EUROPEAN NATIONS.

FIRSTLY, ISRAEL WILL MAINTAIN COMPLETE CONTROL OVER THE GAZA STRIP FROM AN EXTERNAL PERSPECTIVE, ENSURING THE PHYSICAL, LEGAL, AND POLITICAL SEPARATION OF GAZA FROM THE WEST BANK, WHILE ALSO PERPETUATING THE RIVALRY BETWEEN FATAH AND HAMAS. IN AN ATTEMPT TO EXERT INFLUENCE OVER HAMAS, ISRAEL HAS ALLOWED FOREIGN FUNDING TO BOLSTER ITS HOLD ON POWER, WHILE PERIODICALLY RESORTING TO MILITARY STRIKES TO LIMIT ITS AUTHORITY AND COMPEL COMPLIANCE WITH ISRAELI DIRECTIVES.

SECONDLY, ISRAEL HAS OPTED TO MANAGE THE CONFLICT WITH THE PALESTINIANS AS A COLLECTIVE ISSUE RATHER THAN SEEKING RESOLUTION. IN PRACTICE, ISRAEL HAS EXPANDED SETTLEMENTS IN THE WEST BANK, EFFECTIVELY ESTABLISHING A UNIFIED SYSTEM OF GOVERNANCE THAT EXTENDS FROM THE JORDAN RIVER TO THE MEDITERRANEAN SEA. CONSEQUENTLY, THE PALESTINIAN AUTHORITY HAS BEEN TRANSFORMED INTO A SUBCONTRACTOR TASKED WITH CONTROLLING THE PALESTINIAN POPULATION IN THE WEST BANK.

FURTHERMORE, ISRAEL HAS MADE SIGNIFICANT EFFORTS TO DIMINISH THE BROADER ISRAELI-ARAB CONFLICT BY ESTABLISHING NORMALIZATION AGREEMENTS WITH ARAB NATIONS AND MARGINALIZING THE PALESTINIANS, RENDERING THEM ISOLATED AND POWERLESS. THE SIGNING OF THE ABRAHAM ACCORDS ESSENTIALLY SIGNIFIED ISRAEL'S DISREGARD FOR THE FATE OF THE PALESTINIANS, LEAVING THEM AT ISRAEL'S MERCY.

HOWEVER, JUST AS ISRAEL'S STRATEGY WAS ON THE CUSP OF ATTAINING ITS PINNACLE OF ACHIEVEMENT, WITH A POTENTIAL NORMALIZATION AGREEMENT WITH SAUDI ARABIA AND THE COMPLETION OF AN ADVANCED BARRIER ENCIRCLING THE GAZA STRIP, EVERYTHING CRUMBLED ON OCTOBER 7TH.

CONSPIRACIES, PROMISES, AND DIVINE SCRIPTURE: EXPLORING THE SIGNIFICANCE OF NILE TO EUPHRATES CLAIM

THE BELIEF IN A JEWISH HOMELAND KNOWN AS THE GREATER ISRAEL DOCTRINE, IS BASED ON A BIBLICAL INTERPRETATION. ACCORDING TO THIS INTERPRETATION, THE BORDERS OF THE ISRAELI STATE ARE SAID TO STRETCH FROM THE NILE RIVER IN EGYPT TO THE EUPHRATES RIVER IN SYRIA AND IRAQ. THIS BELIEF CAN BE FOUND INSCRIBED AT THE ENTRANCE TO THE KNESSET, THE ISRAELI PARLIAMENT, AND IS ALSO TAUGHT IN SCHOOL CURRICULA. THE BIBLICAL REFERENCE COMES FROM THE COVENANT THAT GOD MADE WITH ABRAHAM, PROMISING HIM AND HIS DESCENDANTS THE LAND FROM THE VALLEY OF EL-ARISH TO THE EUPHRATES RIVER.

ACCORDING TO THE ZIONIST INTERPRETATION OF THE TORAH, AS IN GENESIS 15:18–21, WHERE GOD'S COVENANT WITH ABRAHAM IS MENTIONED:

ON THAT DAY GOD MADE A COVENANT WITH ABRAM, SAYING, "I WILL GIVE THIS LAND TO YOUR DESCENDANTS FROM THE VALLEY OF EL-ARISH TO THE GREAT RIVER, THE EUPHRATES RIVER. THE LAND OF THE KENITES AND THE KENIZZITES, AND THE KADMONITES, AND THE HITTITES, AND THE PERIZZITES, AND THE REPHAIMS, AND THE AMORITES, AND THE CANAANITES, AND THE GIRGASHITES. AND THE JEBUSITES."

IN GENESIS 15:18, ON THAT DAY THE LORD MADE A COVENANT WITH ABRAHAM, SAYING: TO YOUR OFFSPRING I WILL GIVE THIS LAND FROM THE RIVER OF EGYPT TO THE GREAT RIVER, THE RIVER EUPHRATES.

BELIEF PUT INTO PLAN!

THE EARLY MANIFESTATION OF THE PLAN BECAME EVIDENT WHEN THEODOR HERZL, THE FOUNDER OF INTERNATIONAL ZIONISM, DISCUSSED THE ISRAELI ENDEAVOR IN 1904. HE EXPLICITLY STATED THAT THE BORDERS OF THE STATE OF ISRAEL EXTEND FROM "THE RIVER EGYPT TO THE EUPHRATES."

THIS SENTIMENT WAS ECHOED BY RABBI FISHMAN IN 1947 DURING HIS TESTIMONY TO THE UNITED NATIONS SPECIAL INVESTIGATION COMMITTEE. THIS PERSPECTIVE REMAINED UNALTERED UNTIL 2014, WHEN ISRAELI ACTIVISTS SHARED A MAP ON THE SOCIAL NETWORKING SITE "FACEBOOK." THEY REFERRED TO IT AS "THE GREATER KINGDOM OF ISRAEL" OR "THE KINGDOM OF DAVID." THE MAP ENCOMPASSES EGYPT, PALESTINE, JORDAN, SYRIA, LEBANON, AND PARTS OF SAUDI ARABIA AND IRAQ.

ZIONIST CORE BELIEF & NOT CONSPIRACY
FROM THE NILE TO THE EUPHRATES IS A ZIONIST CORE BELIEF, EVEN IF THEY DO NOT ACKNOWLEDGE IT TO THE WORLD IN THE OPEN!

WHO CAN FORGET THE TROUBLE SURROUNDING THE 10 AGORAS? WHICH CENTERED AROUND A THEORY PRODUCED BY YASSER ARAFAT, THE LATE CHAIRMAN OF THE PLO, DURING A SPECIAL MEETING OF THE UN SECURITY COUNCIL IN GENEVA ON MAY 25, 1990.

DURING THE SESSION, ARAFAT ASSERTED THAT THE FRONT SIDE OF THE ISRAELI TEN COIN AGORA FEATURED A MAP OF GREATER ISRAEL, SYMBOLIZING THE ZIONIST MOVEMENT'S ASPIRATIONS FOR EXPANSION.

ARAFAT USED A RESEARCH PAPER BY GWEN ROWLEY FROM THE UNIVERSITY OF SHEFFIELD, TITLED "A BRIEF ASSESSMENT: EVOLVING PERSPECTIVES ON THE LIMITS OF ISRAEL'S TERRITORY," TO SUPPORT HIS ARGUMENTS. IN THIS PAPER, ROWLEY EXPLORES THE QUESTION OF WHAT THE ISRAELITES CONSIDERED AS THE ULTIMATE BOUNDARIES OF THE PROMISED LAND. AS PART OF HER INVESTIGATION, ROWLEY INCLUDES A MAP OF THE MIDDLE EAST WITH AN OUTLINE BASED ON THE PATTERN FOUND ON THE CONTEMPORARY 10 AGORA COIN.

ACCORDING TO ROWLEY, THE 10 AGORA COIN SUGGESTS THAT ISRAEL MAY HAVE BROADER REGIONAL AMBITIONS, AS IT DEPICTS AN AREA THAT EXTENDS TO INCLUDE PRESENT-DAY AMMAN, BEIRUT, BAGHDAD, DAMASCUS, AND PARTS OF SAUDI ARABIA.

ARAFAT'S ALLEGATIONS IN GENEVA SPARKED WIDESPREAD GLOBAL MEDIA COVERAGE AT THE TIME.

THE INITIAL DESIGN WAS CONCEIVED BY NATHAN KARP FOR THE 100 SHEKEL COIN, OFFICIALLY RELEASED BY THE BANK OF ISRAEL ON MAY 2, 1984. FOLLOWING THE TRANSITION FROM THE OLD SHEKEL COIN TO THE NEW SHEKEL IN SEPTEMBER 1985, THE DESIGN WAS REPLICATED ON THE NEW 10 AGORA COIN, EQUIVALENT TO THE VALUE OF 100 SHEKELS. FURTHERMORE, THIS DESIGN WAS ALSO ADOPTED AS AN EMBLEM REPRESENTING THE BANK OF ISRAEL.

THE POWER OF FAITH: EXPLORING THE RESILIENCE OF PALESTINIANS

THE PICTURES AND VIDEOS COMING OUT OF THE GAZA GENOCIDE ARE TRULY GRUESOME. EVEN WITH THE HORROR WE SEE, IT IS INSPIRING TO WITNESS THE RESILIENCE AND FAITH DISPLAYED BY THE PEOPLE OF GAZA. THIS POWERFUL NARRATIVE HAS GAINED TRACTION ON TIKTOK, WITH NUMEROUS INDIVIDUALS EXPRESSING THEIR ADMIRATION FOR THIS UNWAVERING ATTITUDE.

ONE PARTICULAR VIDEO SHOWCASES A WOMAN WALKING ALONGSIDE HER RELATIVE AMIDST A LANDSCAPE OF DEBRIS, SURROUNDED BY CONCRETE BLOCKS. SHE IMPARTS TO HIM THAT AS LONG AS THEY REMAIN PATIENT AND HOLD ONTO THEIR FAITH, ALLAH WILL GRANT THEM THE ABILITY TO REBUILD THEIR LIVES, STRONGER AND MORE PROSPEROUS THAN EVER BEFORE.

AFTER PRAISING GOD, SHE ASSURES HIM THAT REGARDLESS OF THE TRIALS THEY FACE, WHETHER IT BE ILLNESS OR THE DESTRUCTION OF THEIR HOME, THEY MUST ALWAYS OFFER GRATITUDE TO ALLAH.

IN A DIFFERENT VIDEO, WE WITNESS A MAN SITUATED IN A SPACIOUS ROOM, SURROUNDED BY A CROWD OF INDIVIDUALS. WITHIN THE VIDEO, HE STRAIGHTFORWARDLY ADVISES PEOPLE AGAINST SHEDDING TEARS AND ENCOURAGES THEM TO REMAIN STRONG. LATER ON, WHEN QUESTIONED ABOUT HIS PERSONAL LOSSES, HE REVEALS THAT HE HAS EXPERIENCED THE TRAGIC DEATHS OF TWO CHILDREN, ONE AGED 22 AND THE OTHER ONLY 3 YEARS OLD, BOTH OCCURRING ON THE SAME DAY. REMARKABLY, HE DOES NOT DISPLAY ANY SIGNS OF ANGER OR GRIEF BUT INSTEAD DEMONSTRATES ACCEPTANCE OF GOD'S WILL

FURTHERMORE, IN ANOTHER TIKTOK VIDEO, WE ENCOUNTER A MAN POSITIONED AMIDST A FIELD OF RUBBLE, FACING A GROUP OF DEMOLISHED BUILDINGS. SURPRISINGLY, HE WEARS A SMILE WHILE ENGAGING IN CONVERSATION WITH ANOTHER INDIVIDUAL. HE EXPRESSES GRATITUDE FOR HIS FAMILY'S SAFETY AND ATTRIBUTES IT TO ALLAH BY KISSING HIS FINGERS AND GESTURING TOWARDS THE SKY.

IS THE PALESTINIAN RESILIENCE CONNECTED TO THEIR FAITH?

THE PALESTINIANS' ISLAMIC FAITH IS FUNDAMENTAL TO THEIR RESILIENCE, THE HEART OF ISLAM IS THE QURAN, AND OFF COURSE THE QURAN IS FULL OF STORIES OF ADVERSITIES AND CALAMITES BEFALLEN MANKIND, THAT MUSLIMS KNOW BY HEART, THE PROPHET HIMSELF (PEACE BE UPON HIM) HAD ENDURED IMMENSELY FOR THE MESSAGE OF GOD TO BE DELIVERED. WHO CAN FORGET CALAMITY THE PROPHET FACED AT EL TAIF? HERE IS A PREVIEW OF HOW HE FACED CALAMITY WITH MERCY.

THE PROPHET EMBARKED ON A JOURNEY FROM MAKKAH TO TAIF WITH THE INTENTION OF SPREADING THE BELIEF IN THE EXISTENCE OF A SINGLE DEITY.

HE ENGAGED IN A MEETING WITH THE LEADERS OF THE THAQEEF TRIBE, THE PROMINENT TRIBE RESIDING IN TAIF. HE CONVEYED THE TEACHINGS OF ISLAM, EMPHASIZING THE WORSHIP OF ONE GOD AND RENOUNCING IDOLATRY.

REGRETTABLY, HIS MESSAGE WAS MET WITH REJECTION AND HE WAS SUBJECTED TO INSULTS. NOT ONLY DID THEY REFUSE TO LEND AN EAR TO HIS MESSAGE, BUT THEY ALSO INCITED THEIR CHILDREN TO PELT HIM WITH STONES AND EXPEL HIM FROM THEIR TOWN. AMIDST THE MOCKERY AND THE PAIN CAUSED BY BLEEDING ANKLES, HE FLED AND SOUGHT REFUGE IN AN ABANDONED ORCHARD.

ALONE, WOUNDED, AND REJECTED, HE (PEACE BE UPON HIM) FOUND SOLACE AS HE RESTED ON A ROCK AND OFFERED PRAYERS TO ALLAH. DISPLAYING IMMENSE COMPASSION AND MERCY, HE DID NOT IMPLORE GOD TO PUNISH THE PEOPLE OF TAIF OR SEEK REVENGE AGAINST THEM.

THE SUPPLICATION UTTERED BY HIM (PEACE BE UPON HIM) AT TAIF HOLDS GREAT SIGNIFICANCE FOR ALL MUSLIMS. IT SERVES AS A REMINDER TO RECITE IT WHENEVER FACED WITH HARDSHIP, INJUSTICE, OR ADVERSITY.

"TO YOU, MY LORD, I COMPLAIN OF MY WEAKNESS, LACK OF SUPPORT, AND THE HUMILIATION I AM MADE TO RECEIVE. MOST COMPASSIONATE AND MERCIFUL, YOU ARE THE LORD OF THE WEAK, AND YOU ARE MY LORD. TO WHOM DO YOU LEAVE ME? TO A DISTANT PERSON WHO RECEIVES ME WITH HOSTILITY? OR TO AN ENEMY YOU HAVE GIVEN POWER OVER ME? AS LONG AS YOU ARE NOT DISPLEASED WITH ME, I DO NOT CARE WHAT I FACE. I WOULD, HOWEVER, BE MUCH HAPPIER WITH YOUR MERCY.

I SEEK REFUGE IN THE LIGHT OF YOUR FACE BY WHICH ALL DARKNESS IS DISPELLED AND BOTH THIS LIFE AND THE LIFE TO COME ARE PUT IN THEIR RIGHT COURSE AGAINST INCURRING YOUR WRATH OR BEING THE SUBJECT OF YOUR ANGER. TO YOU I SUBMIT, UNTIL I EARN YOUR PLEASURE. EVERYTHING IS POWERLESS WITHOUT YOUR SUPPORT."

AT THAT PARTICULAR MOMENT, ANGEL JIBREEL APPROACHED PROPHET MUHAMMAD AND INFORMED HIM THAT IF HE DESIRED, GOD COULD COMMAND AN ANGEL TO CAUSE THE TWO MOUNTAINS SURROUNDING THE INHABITANTS OF TAIF TO COLLAPSE, OBLITERATING THEM.

HOW DID PROPHET MUHAMMAD (PEACE BE UPON HIM) RESPOND TO THOSE WHO INSULTED AND HURLED STONES AT HIM? HE (PEACE BE UPON HIM) CHOSE MERCY OVER VIOLENCE. HE DID NOT SUCCUMB TO ANGER OR HATRED. INSTEAD OF SEEKING VENGEANCE AGAINST THE PEOPLE OF TAIF, HE EXPRESSED HIS HOPE TO ANGEL JIBREEL THAT GOD WOULD RAISE FUTURE GENERATIONS FROM AMONG THEM WHO WOULD WORSHIP ALLAH

WHEN WE LOOK AT TAIF TODAY, WE CAN TRULY APPRECIATE THE VISION, PATIENCE, AND COMPASSION OF OUR PROPHET. PRESENTLY, TAIF IS HOME TO A POPULATION OF 1,200,000 INDIVIDUALS, PREDOMINANTLY MUSLIM. IT SERVES AS THE SUMMER CAPITAL OF SAUDI ARABIA AND IS RENOWNED FOR ITS GRAPES, POMEGRANATES, FIGS, ROSES, AND HONEY. THOSE RESIDING IN SAUDI ARABIA OFTEN VISIT TAIF FOR ITS COOLER CLIMATE AND THE BREATHTAKING SCENERY OF ITS MOUNTAINS.

OCTOBER 7TH: A DAY OF DEFIANCE FOR PALESTINE AND DECEPTION BY NETANYAHU

Hamas's infiltration into Israel on the 7th of October had a profound impact on the political landscape of the Middle East. It reintroduced the Palestinians into the considerations of regional actors and shattered any illusion that their interests could be disregarded.

However, this incursion came at a devastating cost. The Israeli offensive in the Gaza Strip resulted in the deaths of at least 31,000 Palestinians, with 44% of them being children. Israel justifies its actions by pointing to Hamas's attack on October 7, specifically highlighting the "mass killing of infants and the deliberate and widespread use of sexual violence as a tactic of warfare."

NETANYAHU AND THE CREATION OF HIS GOVERNMENT

THE ISRAELI GOVERNMENT UNDER PRIME MINISTER BENJAMIN NETANYAHU IS A NATIONALIST, EXCLUSIONIST, AND FAR-RIGHT ADMINISTRATION, IT IS THE MOST EXTREMIST GOVERNMENT BEYOND RECOGNITION, THE FIRST OF ITS KIND IN ISRAELI HISTORY.

RIGHT AFTER NEWLY IMPLEMENTED POLICIES OF NETANYAHU'S GOVERNING COALITION, MASSIVE PROTESTS IN TEL AVIV WERE SPARKED, WITH APPROXIMATELY 80,000 DEMONSTRATORS TAKING TO THE STREETS. THE MAIN FOCUS OF THESE PROTESTS HAS BEEN THE GOVERNMENT'S PROPOSED REFORMS TO THE JUDICIAL SYSTEM, WHICH ARE SEEN AS A THREAT TO THE COUNTRY'S DEMOCRACY AND THE PRINCIPLE OF SEPARATION OF POWERS. HOWEVER, THE CONSEQUENCES OF THESE POLICIES EXTEND BEYOND DOMESTIC CONCERNS.

IT WAS NETANYAHU'S SIXTH TERM AS THE LEADER OF THE COUNTRY, BUT IT IS NOT JUST ABOUT HIM. THE SHIFT TO THE RIGHT IN ISRAELI POLITICS HAS BEEN HAPPENING FOR A WHILE, ALONG WITH DECADES OF POLICIES THAT EFFECTIVELY ANNEX THE OCCUPIED WEST BANK AND PROMOTE JEWISH SUPREMACY. WHAT SETS THIS APART IS HOW OPENLY THESE IDEAS ARE EXPRESSED IN THE COALITION GUIDELINES OF THE NEW GOVERNMENT AND BY INFLUENTIAL MINISTERS REGARDING THE CORE PRINCIPLES OF GOVERNANCE.

ISRAEL'S PARLIAMENTARY SYSTEM, CHARACTERIZED BY NUMEROUS FRAGMENTED PARTIES, HAD RESULTED IN THE DOWNFALL OF GOVERNING COALITIONS AND ELECTORAL INSTABILITY, AS EVIDENCED BY THE OCCURRENCE OF FIVE NATIONAL ELECTIONS SINCE 2019. THE FORMATION OF THE "CHANGE" GOVERNMENT IN 2021 AIMED TO UNITE OPPOSING PARTIES AND REMOVE NETANYAHU FROM POWER. HOWEVER, THAT COALITION DISSOLVED DURING THE SUMMER, LEADING TO SUBSEQUENT ELECTIONS WHERE

NETANYAHU MANAGED TO FORM A COALITION WITH ULTRA-ORTHODOX AND RELIGIOUS ZIONIST PARTIES, ULTIMATELY RECLAIMING HIS POSITION AS THE LEADER OF AN EVEN MORE RADICAL EXTREMIST GOVERNMENT. THE INITIAL ACTIONS TAKEN BY THE NATIONAL SECURITY MINISTER, ITAMAR BEN GVIR OF THE JEWISH POWER PARTY, INDICATED A PROVOCATIVE STANCE. HIS POLITICAL IDEOLOGY DRAWS INSPIRATION FROM THE LATE RADICAL ICONOCLAST RABBI MEIR KAHANE. BEN GVIR HAS ASSUMED A POSITION THAT IS SPECIFICALLY SUITED TO OVERSEE BOTH THE POLICE WITHIN ISRAEL AND THE OCCUPIED WEST BANK. IN A HIGHLY CONTENTIOUS MOVE, HE HAD ALREADY VISITED THE TEMPLE MOUNT IN JERUSALEM. ADDITIONALLY, HE HAD INSTRUCTED THE POLICE TO REMOVE ANY PALESTINIAN FLAG DISPLAYED IN PUBLIC SPACES, A DECISION THAT RAISED QUESTIONS ABOUT ITS LEGALITY.

THERE IS ALSO BEZALEL SMOTRICH, WHO SERVES AS THE FINANCE MINISTER. AS THE LEADER OF THE RELIGIOUS ZIONISM PARTY, HE IS A SETTLER KNOWN FOR HIS RADICALISM. HE HAS ALREADY TAKEN CONTROL OF CUSTOMS REVENUES THAT RIGHTFULLY BELONG TO THE PALESTINIAN AUTHORITY, WHICH HE REFERS TO AS A "TERROR-ABETTING BODY" THAT HE BELIEVES SHOULD BE DISMANTLED. ADDITIONALLY, HE WIELDS NEWFOUND POWERS THAT GRANT HIM AUTHORITY OVER THE OCCUPATION OF THE WEST BANK THROUGH A POSITION SPECIALLY TAILORED FOR HIM WITHIN THE DEFENSE MINISTRY.

THE COALITION HAD AN AGREEMENT THAT SET OUT THE NEW GOVERNMENT'S GUIDELINES. THOUGH IT WAS NOT LEGALLY BINDING, IT STATES PLAINLY ITS IDEOLOGY: "THE JEWISH PEOPLE HAVE AN EXCLUSIVE AND INALIENABLE RIGHT OVER ALL AREAS OF THE LAND OF ISRAEL. THE GOVERNMENT WILL PROMOTE AND DEVELOP THE SETTLEMENT OF ALL PARTS OF THE LAND OF ISRAEL — IN THE GALILEE, THE NEGEV, THE GOLAN AND JUDEA AND SAMARIA," THE LATTER REFERRING TO THE OCCUPIED WEST BANK.

IT IS BECOMING MORE AND MORE EVIDENT THAT ISRAEL'S FAR-RIGHT AND ULTRA-ORTHODOX LEADERS ARE USING THE PRETEXT OF WAR TO ADVANCE THEIR PRE-WAR OBJECTIVES. THEIR AIM IS TO TRANSFORM ISRAEL, WHICH IS CURRENTLY A PREDOMINANTLY LIBERAL AND SECULAR DEMOCRACY, INTO A MORE RELIGIOUS, NATIONALIST, AND LESS TOLERANT EXTREMIST SOCIETY.

IT IS HIGHLY QUESTIONABLE WHETHER ANY SIGNIFICANT CHANGES WILL OCCUR ONCE THIS CRISIS COMES TO AN END. FOR INSTANCE, BEN-GVIR HAD ALREADY SCHEDULED HIS DISTRIBUTION OF FIREARMS PRIOR TO THE OUTBREAK OF THE CONFLICT, REFLECTING HIS DELUSIONS OF POWER FOR PATRIOTIC JEWISH ISRAELIS WHO WISH TO DOMINATE THE "ENEMIES OF THE STATE".

NETANYAHU HAS CONSISTENTLY PURSUED RIGHT-WING POLICIES THROUGHOUT HIS TIME IN OFFICE. HOWEVER, AS HIS TENURE HAS PROLONGED, IT IS EVIDENT THAT HIS PRIMARY FOCUS HAS SHIFTED TOWARDS MAINTAINING HIS POSITION OF POWER. THIS POSES A SIGNIFICANT PROBLEM.

HE HAS LOST THE SUPPORT OF THE MAJORITY OF THE POLITICAL ESTABLISHMENT, INCLUDING THE CENTER RIGHT, DUE TO HIS UNWILLINGNESS TO TOLERATE ANY SIGNIFICANT COMPETITION WITHIN HIS OWN LIKUD PARTY AND HIS REFUSAL TO STEP DOWN AFTER BEING CHARGED. AS A RESULT, LIKUD IS NOW FILLED WITH INDIVIDUALS WHO ARE ONLY VALUED FOR THEIR LOYALTY TO NETANYAHU. THE ONLY PARTIES WILLING TO ALIGN WITH NETANYAHU'S GOVERNMENT ARE THOSE ON THE FAR RIGHT AND THE ULTRA-ORTHODOX, AS HE IS WILLING TO MEET THEIR DEMANDS AT ANY COST IN ORDER TO MAINTAIN HIS HOLD ON POWER.

ON 21 NOVEMBER 2019, NETANYAHU WAS OFFICIALLY CHARGED WITH FRAUD AND BREACH OF TRUST IN CASES 1000 AND 2000, AND WITH FRAUD, BREACH OF TRUST, AND RECEIVING BRIBES IN CASE 4000.

BOTH THE EXTREME RIGHT AND THE ULTRA-ORTHODOX FACTIONS ARE FULLY COGNIZANT THAT THEIR TENURE IN POWER IS LIKELY TO COME TO AN END SOON. CONSEQUENTLY, THEY ARE DETERMINED TO EFFECT AS MUCH TRANSFORMATION ON THE GROUND AS THEY CAN WHILE THEY STILL POSSESS THE ABILITY TO DO SO. HOWEVER, IF THEY ARE GRANTED SUFFICIENT TIME — AND NETANYAHU HAS HIS OWN MOTIVATIONS FOR AFFORDING THEM THAT OPPORTUNITY — THEY COULD POTENTIALLY RESHAPE THE LANDSCAPE OF ISRAEL IN A MANNER THAT CANNOT BE REVERSED.

NETANYAHU DECEPTION AND FALSE FLAG

ACCORDING TO THE AP, THE ISRAELI MILITARY HAD PRIOR KNOWLEDGE OF HAMAS' INTENTION TO CARRY OUT AN ASSAULT ON ISRAELI TERRITORY MORE THAN A YEAR BEFORE THE OPERATION ON OCTOBER 7TH, WHICH RESULTED IN THE LOSS OF HUNDREDS OF LIVES. THIS REPORT FROM THE NEW YORK TIMES HIGHLIGHTS A PATTERN WHERE SENIOR ISRAELI COMMANDERS EITHER DISREGARDED OR DOWNPLAYED THE WARNINGS REGARDING HAMAS' PLANS. THE TIMES FURTHER REVEALS THAT ISRAELI OFFICIALS POSSESSED A COMPREHENSIVE 40-PAGE BATTLE PLAN, KNOWN AS "JERICHO WALL," OUTLINING A HYPOTHETICAL ATTACK BY HAMAS ON SOUTHERN ISRAELI COMMUNITIES.

A FALSE FLAG OPERATION IS AN ACT COMMITTED WITH THE INTENT OF DISGUISING THE ACTUAL SOURCE OF RESPONSIBILITY AND PINNING BLAME ON ANOTHER PARTY.

NETANYAHU AND EXTREMIST MEMBERS OF HIS GOVERNMENT HAD VITAL INFORMATION ABOUT THE ATTACK, YET THEY DID NOTHIN TO STOP IT!

WHY YOU MIGHT ASK? SIMPLY, BECAUSE IT SERVES THEIR AGENDA OF EXPANSION OF TERRITORY, AND THE COMPLETE TRANSFORMATION OF THE STATE OF ISRAEL. REMEMBER THE EXTREMIST COALITION'S MEMORANDUM?! THESE PEOPLE WANT TO EXPAND, THEY ALLOWED THE ATTACK TO HAPPEN, SO THAT THEY HAVE THE CASUS BELLI TO RAGE WAR AND FULFILL THEIR DREAMS OF SUPREMACY!

A CASUS BELLI IS AN ACT OR AN EVENT THAT EITHER PROVOKES OR IS USED TO JUSTIFY A WAR. A CASUS BELLI INVOLVES DIRECT OFFENSES OR THREATS AGAINST THE NATION DECLARING THE WAR.

WE HAVE TO WAKE UP FROM THIS DECEPTION, WE ARE BEING MANIPULATED TO THE LARGEST EXTENT, IT IS UNBELIEVABLE.

SILENCING THE TRUTH: ZIONISTS' DICTATION OF WESTERN MEDIA

Numerous public figures who have lost their jobs or faced disciplinary actions for expressing their solidarity with the Palestinians.

Here are a few notable figures who seem to have encountered similar immediate repercussions for speaking the truth:

Melissa Barrera

The actress was removed from the cast of Scream 7 after several of her social media updates where she described the events in Gaza as "genocide," "ethnic cleansing," and "similar to a concentration camp."

"Western media only shows the [Israeli] side. Why do they do that, I will let you deduce for yourself," she <u>wrote</u> in October. "We don't need more hate. No Islamophobia. No antisemitism."

A REPRESENTATIVE FROM SPYGLASS MEDIA GROUP, THE COMPANY RESPONSIBLE FOR THE FILM SCREAM, LATER INFORMED VARIETY: SPYGLASS' STANCE IS UNEQUIVOCALLY CLEAR: WE HAVE ZERO TOLERANCE FOR ANTISEMITISM OR THE INCITEMENT OF HATE IN ANY FORM, INCLUDING FALSE REFERENCES TO GENOCIDE, ETHNIC CLEANSING, HOLOCAUST DISTORTION OR ANYTHING THAT FLAGRANTLY CROSSES THE LINE INTO HATE SPEECH."

MELISSA SUBSEQUENTLY <u>WROTE</u> ON INSTAGRAM, AND PER ROLLING STONE. "AS A LATINA, A PROUD MEXICANA, I FEEL THE RESPONSIBILITY OF HAVING A PLATFORM THAT ALLOWS ME THE PRIVILEGE OF BEING HEARD, AND THEREFORE I HAVE TRIED TO USE IT TO RAISE AWARENESS ABOUT ISSUES I CARE ABOUT, AND TO LEND MY VOICE TO THOSE IN NEED."

"I CONDEMN ANTISEMITISM AND ISLAMOPHOBIA. I CONDEMN HATE AND PREJUDICE OF ANY KIND AGAINST ANY GROUP OF PEOPLE" MELISSA WROTE

SUSAN SARANDON

SUSAN WAS RELEASED FROM HER CONTRACT WITH THE UNITED TALENT AGENCY AFTER PARTICIPATING IN A PRO-PALESTINIAN DEMONSTRATION IN NEW YORK CITY. SHE EXPRESSED HER STRONG OPPOSITION TO BOTH ANTISEMITISM AND ISLAMOPHOBIA.

SHE REPORTEDLY SAID, "THERE ARE A LOT OF PEOPLE AFRAID OF BEING JEWISH AT THIS TIME, AND ARE GETTING A TASTE OF WHAT IT FEELS LIKE TO BE A MUSLIM IN THIS COUNTRY, SO OFTEN SUBJECTED TO VIOLENCE."

BELLA HADID

"MY FAMILY HAS FELT TO BE IN DANGER. BUT I CANNOT BE SILENCED ANY LONGER. FEAR IS NOT AN OPTION. THE PEOPLE AND CHILDREN OF PALESTINE, ESPECIALLY IN GAZA, CANNOT AFFORD OUR SILENCE. WE ARE NOT BRAVE — THEY ARE," BELLA REPORTEDLY WROTE IN HER FIRST STATEMENT ON INSTAGRAM

THE PALESTINIAN-DUTCH MODEL AND HER SISTER GIGI HADID HAVE BOTH FACED DEATH THREATS AFTER EXPRESSING THEIR SOLIDARITY WITH PALESTINIANS.

"I HAD SO MANY COMPANIES STOP WORKING WITH ME," BELLA SAID IN 2022 REGARDING HER PREVIOUS SUPPORT OF PALESTINIANS. "I HAD FRIENDS THAT COMPLETELY DROPPED ME, LIKE EVEN FRIENDS I HAD BEEN HAVING DINNER WITH AT THEIR HOME ON FRIDAY NIGHTS, FOR SEVEN YEARS, LIKE NOW JUST WON'T LET ME AT THEIR HOUSE ANYMORE."

IT SEEMS THAT ANYONE OPPOSED TO ISRAEL OR ZIONISM IS BRANDED AS ANTI-SEMITIC! LETS DISCOVER WHAT THAT REALLY MEANS TO BE ANTISEMITIC!

WHAT IS ANTISEMITISM?

"ANTISEMITISM IS A CERTAIN PERCEPTION OF JEWS, WHICH MAY BE EXPRESSED AS HATRED TOWARD JEWS. RHETORICAL AND PHYSICAL MANIFESTATIONS OF ANTISEMITISM ARE DIRECTED TOWARD JEWISH COMMUNITY INSTITUTIONS AND RELIGIOUS FACILITIES."

THE ISRAELI GOVERNMENT'S ONGOING MENTION OF (HOLOCAUST RELATED) HISTORIC HATRED TOWARDS JEWS DOES NOT GIVE THE ISRAELI GOVERNMENT A FREE PASS TO KILL NUMEROUS CIVILIANS (MAINLY WOMEN AND CHILDREN) IN GAZA AS A RESPONSE TO THE HAMAS ATTACK ON OCTOBER 7TH.

ANTISEMITISM IS BEING WIDELY USED BY THE ISRAELI GOVERNMENT AS A POLITICAL TOOL!

IN FACT: THERE HAVE BEEN NUMEROUS INSTANCES WHERE ISRAEL HAS BEEN COMPARED TO THE NAZIS, WHETHER IN PROTESTS, ON SOCIAL MEDIA, OR BY WORLD LEADERS. ON OCTOBER 10, THE PRESIDENT OF COLOMBIA, GUSTAVO PETRO, EXPRESSED ON HIS X (FORMERLY TWITTER) ACCOUNT THAT "GAZA IS NOW AS DEVASTATED, IF NOT MORE SO, THAN THE WARSAW GHETTO" AND THAT AFTER "THE JEWISH AND SOCIALIST UPRISING, THAT CONCENTRATION CAMP WAS DESTROYED BY NAZI BARBARISM."

FROM THE NILE TO GAZA: EGYPT'S CRUCIAL ROLE IN ASSISTING THE PALESTINIAN PEOPLE

FOR THE PAST FEW DECADES, CAIRO HAS CONSISTENTLY EMPHASIZED ITS NATIONAL STANCE ON THE PALESTINIAN MATTER, VIEWING IT AS A CENTRAL ISSUE IN THE REGION. THIS STANCE IS ROOTED IN SEVERAL KEY PRINCIPLES, INCLUDING THE BELIEF THAT THE ONLY VIABLE SOLUTION TO THE PALESTINIAN ISSUE IS THROUGH A TWO-STATE RESOLUTION AND THE CREATION OF AN INDEPENDENT PALESTINIAN STATE. THIS STATE WOULD BE ESTABLISHED ON THE BORDERS OF JUNE 4, 1967, WITH EAST JERUSALEM SERVING AS ITS CAPITAL. CAIRO ALSO MAINTAINS STRONG POSITIONS AGAINST UNILATERAL MEASURES THAT IMPEDE THE ESTABLISHMENT OF A PALESTINIAN STATE, SUCH AS SETTLEMENTS AND ISRAELI ACTIONS IN JERUSALEM. ADDITIONALLY, CAIRO SUPPORTS THE JUST RIGHTS OF THE PALESTINIAN PEOPLE, PARTICULARLY THEIR RIGHT TO RETURN HOME.

THIS CREED BECAME MORE EVIDENT DURING THE RECENT GENOCIDE IN THE GAZA STRIP, WHICH HAS BEEN ONGOING SINCE LAST OCTOBER. THIS GENOCIDE HAS HAD CONSEQUENCES AT THE SECURITY, HUMANITARIAN, AND POLITICAL LEVELS, AFFECTING THE WHOLE OF THE MIDDLE EAST. IN LIGHT OF EGYPT'S HISTORICAL RESPONSIBILITY, PIVOTAL ROLE, AND NATIONAL DUTIES, IT TOOK THE INITIATIVE TO SUPPORT THE PALESTINIAN PEOPLE. EGYPT HAS WORKED WITH TREMENDOUS EFFORT TO PRESENT A PRACTICAL AND EFFECTIVE SOLUTION THAT WOULD CONTRIBUTE TO ENDING THE GENOCIDE IN THE GAZA STRIP, ACHIEVING A CEASEFIRE, AND INITIATING A POLITICAL PROCESS AIMED AT ATTAINING THE ULTIMATE GOAL — **THE TWO-STATE SOLUTION**.

LET'S NOT OVERLOOK THE EGYPTIAN PRESIDENT'S EFFORTS TO COUNTER WHAT COULD BE DESCRIBED AS AN ENDEAVOR TO "ELIMINATE" OR "LIQUIDATE" THE RIGHTS OF THE PALESTINIANS. HE EMPHASIZED THAT WHILE EGYPT HAS WELCOMED HUNDREDS OF THOUSANDS OF CITIZENS FROM COUNTRIES LIKE SYRIA AND SUDAN IN RECENT YEARS, THE SITUATION IS COMPLETELY DIFFERENT FOR THE RESIDENTS OF THE GAZA STRIP. ANY ATTEMPT TO MOVE THE GAZAN POPULATION WILL DEFINITELY END ANY ATTEMPT FOR A TWO-STATE SOLUTION, BECAUSE IF A FORCED DISPLACEMENT WERE TO BE FORCED ON THE PALESTINIAN PEOPLE, THEY WILL HAVE NO MEANS OF RETURNING BACK , AND THEREFORE SURRENDER ANY DREAM OF A PALESTINIAN STATE. ALLOWING THEM TO LEAVE WOULD ONLY SERVE THE INTERESTS OF CERTAIN ISRAELI FACTIONS THAT SEEK TO PERMANENTLY END THE EXISTENCE OF THE GAZA STRIP, AND ELIMINATE THE DREAM OF A PALESTINIAN STATE.

THE CITY OF CAIRO HAS BEEN A VENUE FOR NUMEROUS NEGOTIATIONS BETWEEN ISRAEL AND THE PALESTINIAN FACTIONS, WITH THE ACTIVE INVOLVEMENT OF QATAR AND THE UNITED STATES OF AMERICA. OVER THE PAST HALF-YEAR, CAIRO HAS WELCOMED SEVERAL WORLD LEADERS, PRIME MINISTERS, FOREIGN MINISTERS, AND REPRESENTATIVES FROM INTERNATIONAL AND REGIONAL ORGANIZATIONS TO DELIBERATE ON STRATEGIES FOR ACHIEVING A TEMPORARY CEASEFIRE, AND END THE ONGOING GENOCIDE IN GAZA.

EGYPT'S EFFORTS ON THE GROUND

EGYPT HAS DEMONSTRATED UNWAVERING COMMITMENT ALSO AT THE HUMANITARIAN LEVEL. THIS COMMITMENT IS EVIDENT THROUGH VARIOUS ACTIONS, INCLUDING ADVOCATING FOR AID, ESTABLISHING TEMPORARY SHELTERS, AND CONDUCTING AIRDROPS OF ASSISTANCE. DESPITE FACING CHALLENGES SUCH AS ISRAELI BOMBINGS AND IMPOSED RESTRICTIONS, EGYPT HAS REMAINED STEADFAST IN ITS DETERMINATION TO FACILITATE AID DELIVERY TO THE GAZA STRIP.

THIS DETERMINATION IS EXEMPLIFIED BY EGYPT'S CONTINUOUS OPERATION OF THE RAFAH CROSSING AND ITS UTILIZATION OF DUAL NATIONALITY DOCUMENTATION TO OVERCOME OBSTACLES. ULTIMATELY, EGYPT HAS EVEN RESORTED TO AIRDROPPING AID INTO THE GAZA STRIP, PROVING ITS DEDICATION TO SUPPORTING THOSE IN NEED.

EGYPTIAN AUTHORITIES ARE ALWAYS WORKING TO PROVIDE MEDICAL TREATMENT TO INJURED PALESTINIANS IN EGYPTIAN HOSPITALS. AT THE SAME TIME, RELIEF PLANES CONTINUE TO ARRIVE AT AL-ARISH INTERNATIONAL AIRPORT, WITH A TOTAL OF 582 PLANES HAVING LANDED SO FAR. ADDITIONALLY, CAIRO IS NEARING COMPLETION OF THE "KHAN YUNIS" CAMP, WHICH IS INTENDED TO ACCOMMODATE THE GROWING NUMBER OF DISPLACED PALESTINIANS FROM THE CENTRAL AND NORTHERN GAZA STRIP.

EGYPT HAS BEEN COMMITTED TO ESTABLISHING A SERIES OF CAMPS TO ADDRESS THIS ISSUE. MOREOVER, CAIRO HAS PRIORITIZED THE ESTABLISHMENT OF A HUMANITARIAN AIR BRIDGE, WITH EGYPTIAN AND JORDANIAN AIRCRAFT CONDUCTING DAILY FLIGHTS TO DELIVER MUCH-NEEDED AID TO THE RESIDENTS OF THE NORTHERN GAZA STRIP. THE AIM IS TO ALLEVIATE THE FAMINE FACED BY THE PALESTINIANS DUE TO THE ISRAELI BLOCKADE HINDERING THE REGULAR AND SUFFICIENT ENTRY OF AID INTO GAZA.

THE TRUTH IS THAT THE CURRENT OUTCOME OF THE RELIEF AND HUMANITARIAN EFFORTS IN THE GAZA STRIP CONDUCTED BY EGYPT IS THE MOST SIGNIFICANT AND EXTENSIVE AMONG ALL OTHER ENDEAVORS MADE BY ARAB AND FOREIGN NATIONS COMBINED!!! APPROXIMATELY 87 PERCENT OF THE AID BROUGHT INTO THE GAZA STRIP SINCE LAST OCTOBER CAN BE ATTRIBUTED TO EGYPT, WITH A TOTAL OF 10,868 TONS OF MEDICINES AND MEDICAL SUPPLIES, AROUND 10,235 TONS OF FUEL, 129,329 TONS OF FOOD, AND 26,364 TONS OF DRINKING WATER DELIVERED THROUGH THE RAFAH CROSSING.

FURTHERMORE, 43,073 TONS OF MEDICAL MATERIALS, ALONG WITH 123 FULLY EQUIPPED AMBULANCES, HAVE ENTERED THE GAZA STRIP VIA RAFAH. THE EGYPTIAN HUMANITARIAN EFFORTS ALSO EXTENDED BEYOND AID OPERATIONS. EGYPTIAN HOSPITALS HAVE ACCOMMODATED 3,706 INJURED PALESTINIANS, ACCOMPANIED BY 6,071 ESCORTS THUS FAR.

War or Theater? Unmasking the Theatrics and Propaganda Between Iran and Israel

Iran conducted an apparent assault on Saturday evening, unleashing approximately 300 attack drones and missiles from its own territory towards Israel. This marks the first direct attack by the Islamic Republic on the Zionist state, causing air raid sirens to blare across Israel early Sunday. The country's military swiftly mobilized to intercept the incoming Iranian projectiles.

Iran unleashed over 300 projectiles which included 170 drones, 30 cruise missiles, and 120 ballistic missiles. Astonishingly, Israeli air defenses managed to intercept a staggering 99% of these incoming threats.

WAS THERE ANY REAL THREAT?

THE TRUTH IS THAT THE CONFLICT STARTED BY A HUGE "PROPAGANDA WAR," AND WAS INITIATED BY BIASED PARTIES ASSOCIATED WITH EITHER IRAN OR ISRAEL. NEARLY ALL OF THOSE REPORTS OF ESCALATION AND REVENGE SERVE PROPAGANDA OBJECTIVES BY IRAN, PARTICULARLY GIVEN THE ONGOING LEAKS FROM BOTH IRAN AND ISRAEL, WHICH CONTAIN THREATS AND REAFFIRM PREPAREDNESS.

THE ASSAULT ITSELF AND THE HUGE PROPAGANDA LEADING UP TO IT SERVE AS COMPONENTS OF INTIMIDATION AND TERROR PROPAGANDA IN THE CONTEXT OF PSYCHOLOGICAL WARFARE. THIS IS PARTICULARLY NOTEWORTHY CONSIDERING THAT THERE WERE SPECULATIONS FROM CERTAIN SOURCES ABOUT IRAN LAUNCHING THE ATTACK ON FRIDAY EVENING, WHICH ULTIMATELY DID NOT OCCUR. NONETHELESS, THESE SPECULATIONS DID EVOKE FEARS WITHIN ISRAEL AND THE UNITED STATES.

IT SEEMS THAT IRAN WAS CONVINCED THAT THE MERE THREATS HAD MORE IMPACT, AND THAT IS TRUE, THE ACTUAL ASSAULT WAS ONLY THEATRICS GIVEN THAT WERE NO TARGETED HITS, I MEAN 99% MAYBE EVEN 99.9% WERE NOT EFFECTIVE.

THIS IS WHAT YAHYA RAHIM SAFAVI, THE MILITARY ADVISOR TO THE IRANIAN LEADER ALI KHAMENEI, HAD TO SAY: "WE CARRIED OUT A SUCCESSFUL PSYCHOLOGICAL AND MEDIA OPERATION AGAINST ISRAEL AND ACHIEVED THE GOAL. IT FRIGHTENED AND TERRIFIED BOTH THE UNITED STATES AND ISRAEL, AND THIS PSYCHOLOGICAL WAR POLITICAL AND MEDIA MATTERS ARE MORE TERRIBLE FOR ISRAEL THAN FIGHTING."

HOSSEIN AMIR-ABDOLLAHIAN, IRAN'S FOREIGN MINISTER, SPOKE IN A MEETING WITH FOREIGN AMBASSADORS IN TEHRAN PRIOR TO THE ATTACK. HERE IS WHAT HE SAID:

WE INFORMED THE US OUR OPERATION AGAINST ISRAEL WILL BE "LIMITED" AND FOR SELF-DEFENSE

WE DON'T SEEK TO EXPAND CONFLICT IN THE REGION

WE HAVE INFORMED THE US WE'LL TARGET ITS BASES IF IRAN IS TARGETED

ABOUT 72 HOURS PRIOR TO THE OPERATION, WE INFORMED OUR NEIGHBOURS AND COUNTRIES IN THE REGION THAT IRAN'S RESPONSE, AS PART OF A LEGITIMATE DEFENCE, WAS CERTAIN AND DEFINITIVE.

THE SECURITY OF NEIGHBORING COUNTRIES IS TOP OF IRAN'S PRIORITIES.

ANALYSTS PROPOSE THAT IRAN'S DRONE STRIKE, WHICH UNFOLDED VERY VERY SLOWLY, WAS STRATEGICALLY DESIGNED TO SHOWCASE ITS POWER WHILE AT THE SAME TIME ALLOWING TIME FOR ISRAELI DEFENSIVE MEASURES TO ACT!!

According to Nishank Motwani, a senior analyst at the Australian Strategic Policy Institute in Washington, DC, it seems that Iran intentionally signaled its attack on Israel to demonstrate its ability to strike using different capabilities. However, this was done to provide an opportunity for de-escalation.

Motwani adds that Tehran had the option to escalate the situation across various fronts, including through the Lebanese armed group Hezbollah, sea attacks, or targeting soft Israeli assets on a global scale, but it didn't.

Biden said that he was convening fellow G7 leaders on Sunday to "coordinate a united diplomatic response" to Iran's attack, in an apparent indication that a military response is not currently on the table.

THE GENOCIDE CONTINUES

THE WAR IN GAZA SEEMS TO HAVE NO END IN SIGHT, WITH THE ISRAELI LEADERSHIP POINTING OUT THE WAR COULD LAST FOR MONTHS. THE MAIN ISSUE HERE SHOULD BE TO END THE HUMAN SUFFERING OF THE GAZAN POPULATION, THE PALESTINIANS ARE WILLING TO NEGOTIATE A TRUCE AND AN EXCHANGE OF HOSTAGES AND PRISONERS. SO WHAT SEEMS TO BE THE ISSUE HERE?

THE PROBLEM LIES WITH THE ISRAELI GOVERNMENT, THERE IS NO DOUBT THAT THE PEOPLE OF ISRAEL ALSO WANT AN END TO THIS WAR, AND THE RETURN OF THE HOSTAGES. THE GOVERNMENT SEEMS TO HAVE OTHER GOALS OR OBJECTIVES IN LINE. THEY TALK ABOUT THE ERADICATION OF HAMAS, BUT IS THAT POSSIBLE? EVEN WITH A HUGE AMOUNT OF CASUALTIES (WOMEN AND CHILDREN INCLUDED), CAN THEY ERADICATE HAMAS, PRESENTLY WE SEE NO SIGN OR CLEAR INDICATION OF THAT!

THE GENOCIDE CAN ONLY BE STOPPED THROUGH DIRECT CONFRONTATION. THE GENOCIDE HAS BEEN PLAYED ALL ALONG LIKE A TEXAS HOLD-THEM GAME OF POKER BY THE ISRAELI EXTREMIST GOVERNMENT, IT IS TIME FOR THE ARABS TO ONCE RAISE A CALL, INSTEAD OF FEARFULLY CALLING EVERY RAISE DONE BY THE ISRAELI COUNTERPART. EXTREMISM CAN NOT BE FOUGHT WITH LENIENCY OR DIPLOMACY AT FIRST. TO END THIS GENOCIDE, THE ARAB NEIGHBORS OF ISRAEL MUST TAKE DRASTIC MEASURES, IF THEY FORGOT ABOUT THE ETHICAL MORALITY OF THE ISSUE AT HAND, THEY MUST CONTEMPLATE THOROUGHLY THE ECONOMIC DISASTROUS SCENARIOS AT HAND. EGYPT AND JORDAN (ALONG WITH THE BACKING OF THE ARAB STATES) SHOULD OCCUPY THE GAZA STRIP. NOW THIS CAN BE DONE BY EITHER A DIRECT REQUEST BY THE PALESTINIAN AUTHORITY CITING THE REASON IS "GENOCIDE", OR IT CAN BE DONE THE RUSSIAN WAY, ANONYMOUS FOOT-SOLDIERS WITH NO FLAG OCCUPYING THE STRIP. (IT HAS BEEN DONE BEFORE, I CITE CRIMEA)

NOW A DIPLOMATIC CAMPAIGN MUST BE HELD AT THE SAME TIME, TO ENSURE THAT IT IS NOT AN ACT OF AGGRESSION, BUT IT IS MERELY AN ACT OF SELF DEFENSE ON BEHALF OF THE PALESTINIAN PEOPLE, THE JOINT-ARAB FORCES WILL NOT EXCEED THE GAZA-STRIP, HOWEVER WILL DEMAND IMMEDIATE CEASE OF FIRE AND A START OF NEGOTIATIONS. ITS TIME FOR THE ARAB COALITION TO RAISE THE STAKES, NOT ONLY FOR THE ETHICAL MORAL ASPECT OF THE WAR (WHICH SHOULD BE ENOUGH), BUT FOR THE SOVEREIGN AND MOST DANGEROUSLY ECONOMIC PERILS OF THIS WAR.

IN THE END, IT IS NOT OUT INTENTION TO CALL FOR WAR, BUT IT IS TIME TO HAVE AN ASSERTIVE ACTION, SOMETIMES THE ANSWER LIES IN THE PLACE YOU ARE MOST AFRAID TO VISIT!